CHESS
SELF-TEACHER

ABOUT THE AUTHOR

Al Horowitz has earned a two-fold reputation as one of the foremost chess players in the United States and as a leading writer on the subject. He has been the United States Open Chess Champion three times and has also been three times a member of the United States World Championship Team. He is the author of over a dozen books on chess and is the founder, editor, and publisher of the magazine, *Chess Review*. He runs a column on chess in the *Saturday Review* and in the New York *Times*. He has also taught university classes and has lectured widely on the techniques of chess.

Among his books are three published in Barnes & Noble Books: *First Book of Chess* (with Fred Reinfeld), *Chess for Beginners : A Picture Guide,* and this volume.

CHESS
SELF-TEACHER

by AL HOROWITZ

PERENNIAL LIBRARY

Harper & Row, Publishers
New York, Cambridge, Philadelphia, San Francisco
London, Mexico City, São Paulo, Singapore, Sydney

CONTENTS

PREFACE

If all books on chess instruction were condensed into a single dictum, it could offer no finer counsel than "play chess." The very act of doing things oneself imparts more practical learning for the time and effort spent than a host of academic theories. This work is founded on that conviction.

The rules of chess are simple. Yet it is surprising how many interpretations, or more correctly misinterpretations, are attributed to the clearest writing. Nearly every day this writer receives the most elementary questions from all over the nation from those who have played chess for a good many years. "Is it legal for me to castle here?" "May I move a King into a square attacked by my opponent's pinned piece?" The *Self-Teacher* will obviate these. The "self-teacher" approach is the positive way of checking and double checking every point raised. A "review" in the form of questions will reaffirm the learner's knowledge, and a "quiz" requiring some original thinking will crystallize it. The answers to the "reviews" and the "quizzes" are given to make assurance doubly sure.

It is with the fond hope that the readers of *Chess Self-Teacher* will direct *their* questions on a higher level that this work is written.

AL HOROWITZ

CHESS
SELF-TEACHER

Lesson I

THE GAME OF CHESS

Chess is a game for two players, who are conventionally called *White* and *Black*. White always makes the first move to begin a game, and thereafter the players move alternately.

The game is played on the familiar chessboard (described below). Each player has 16 pieces (described below). The pieces used by Black are colored black or red; those used by White may be white, a shade of white, or the natural color of boxwood.

The object of play is to capture one particular enemy piece, the *king*. When the king is attacked and cannot possibly escape, he is not actually removed from the board; he is said to be *checkmated*, and the game ends as a win for the opponent. A move that attacks the king is called a *check*, and on making such a move the player customarily warns his opponent by saying "Check!" This warning is not compulsory under the rules; if a player fails to notice that his king is checked and makes some move that does not stop the check, he must simply retract that move. To leave the king in check is illegal.

If a player, at his turn to move, has no legal move, but his king is not in check, the position is *stalemate*. A stalemate is a drawn game. A draw may also come about in other ways, as will be explained later.

THE CHESSBOARD

The chessboard (identical to the checkerboard) is a square composed of 64 smaller squares, which are colored alternately light and dark (see Diagram I-1). These small squares are often referred

BLACK

WHITE

I-1   **The Chessboard**

to as *white* and *black,* though these two colors are not actually used on most of the boards manufactured. The squares are better called *light* and *dark* so as to reserve White and Black exclusively for the names of the players.

The players sit at opposite sides of the board, which must be so placed that each player finds a light square in the corner nearest his right hand.

In the printed diagram, Black's side of the board is always placed at the top, White's at the bottom.

THE PIECES

Initial Array. To begin a game, the 32 pieces are placed on the board as shown in Diagram I-2. Study this diagram to learn

I-2　　　　　　　　　　　**Initial Array**

the conventional symbols that are used for the pieces in printing.

The pieces are shown to the right. The *rook* is sometimes called *castle*. The word *piece* is often used to designate a chessman other than a *pawn*. Observe in Diagram I-2 that all the *pieces* are set up on the row nearest the player; in front of them is a row of eight *pawns*. The *king* and *queen* go on the two central squares of the first row. The traditional rule as to which goes where is "queen on her color," meaning that the Black queen goes on the dark square, the White queen on the light square. The central pieces are flanked (going outwards) by *bishops, knights,* and *rooks.*

	WHITE	BLACK
Rook		
Knight		
Bishop		
Queen		
King		
Pawn		

Different manufacturers use different designs for their chess pieces. The printed symbols are based on the *Staunton pattern,* favored in Britain and the United States and used for turned box-wood sets. Plastic chessmen are usually modeled on severely simplified designs, but certain features are preserved so that each piece can be identified:

The king is the tallest piece. He may have a cross or knob at the top.

The queen is second tallest. She may have a crown with points.

The pawn is the shortest piece.

The bishop is intermediate in size and design between the queen and pawn. He may have a cleft in his side.

The rook has a cylindrical body, usually castellated at top.

The knight has a horse's head.

The following abbreviations are used in designating the pieces:

King	K	Bishop	B
Queen	Q	Pawn	P
Rook	R	Knight	Kt or N or S

(N is phonetic for knight, S is for the German *Springer.*)

THE MOVES

Each of the six different kinds of pieces has powers of movement different from those of the others. The first step in learning chess is to learn "the moves."

Capture. The capturing move in chess is *not* (as in checkers) a jump. Instead, the capturing piece replaces the captured piece on its square, and the captured piece is removed from the board. Another way of putting it is that, if a piece can move to a given square, then it can capture an enemy piece standing on that square (with the exception of the capturing moves of the pawn). (See pp. 8-10.)

The King. The king may move in any direction to an adjacent square, as shown in Diagram I-3, always provided that he does not move into check. The king thus commands a maximum of 8 squares, which is cut to 5 if he stands on a side of the board and to 3 if he is in a corner.

I-3   **The King Move**

The Rook. The rook moves parallel to the sides of the board any distance along an unobstructed line of squares (Diagram I-4). Thus a rook may command as many as 14 squares.

BLACK

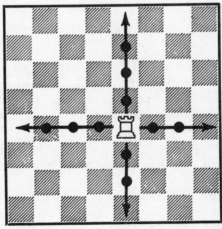

WHITE

I-4   **The Rook Move**

Castling. Once in a game (if at all) a player may make a move called *castling*. This is a compound move by the king and one rook. Both pieces must stand on their original squares. To castle, move the king two squares toward the rook, then move the

BLACK

WHITE

I-5   Castling

rook to the square leaped over by the king. In Diagram I-5, the White pieces show how castling is executed on either side; the Black pieces show the final positions of the two pieces after castling on either side.

Castling is legal only if all the following conditions are met:

(a) The squares on the line between king and rook are vacant.

(b) The king and rook stand on their original squares and neither has moved at all during the game.

(c) The king is not in check.

(d) Neither the square leaped over by the king nor the one to which he moves is commanded by an enemy piece.

The Bishop. The bishop moves any distance along an unobstructed diagonal line of squares. Thus he commands a maximum of 13 squares. (Diagram I-6)

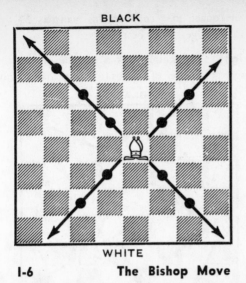

1-6   **The Bishop Move**

Notice that a bishop is always tied to squares of one color. Each player begins the game with one *white* or *light* bishop and one *black* or *dark*.

The Queen. The queen combines the powers of the rook and bishop. That is, she can move any distance along an unobstructed line of squares, parallel to the side of the board or diagonally (Diagram

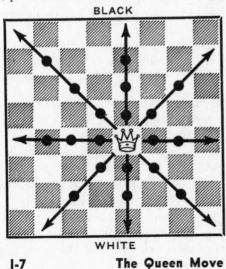

1-7   **The Queen Move**

I-7). Thus the queen may command as many as 27 squares and is consequently the strongest piece on the board.

The Knight. The knight has a peculiar move, best described as "to the nearest square of opposite color that is not adjacent."

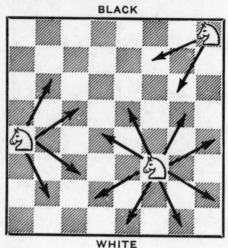

BLACK

WHITE

I-8   **The Knight Move**

He moves in the shape of an inverted L. Study Diagram I-8 and learn this move as a unity, not as a combination of two steps at right angles ("a slither and a side step"). The knight commands at the most 8 squares; in a corner, only 2.

The knight goes from *point to point,* not along a line of squares. Consequently he cannot be obstructed by neighboring pieces; the knight leaps right over them. He is the only piece having this peculiarity.

The Pawn. The pawn is the only piece that may never move backward. Its noncapturing move is straight ahead. From its initial position, it has the option of moving ahead one square or of leaping this square to the one beyond, as shown in the lower left corner of Diagram I-9. Once it has left its initial post, it may no longer make a double jump but must plod on one square at a time.

The pawn is the only piece that captures in a way different from its noncapturing move. It captures to the square diagonally adjacent and forward. Thus in Diagram I-9 the White pawn (lower right) may capture the Black knight or the pawn may move ahead one square, as shown.

8 • The Game of Chess

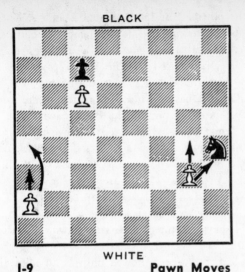

I-9   **Pawn Moves**

Since a pawn captures diagonally, not straight ahead, it can be blocked by an enemy piece standing in front of it. In the upper part of Diagram I-9 are a Black and a White pawn, face to face. The pawns are *stopped*—neither can advance.

Capture *En Passant*. A White and a Black pawn advancing on adjacent lines must sooner or later meet diagonally, so that

BLACK

I-10   ***En Passant***

each attacks the other. It is felt to be undesirable to let a pawn pass by an enemy pawn through the double jump without attack. Hence a special rule allows capture *en passant* ("in passing"). The situation is illustrated in Diagram I-10. The White pawn has reached the 5th row away from the White side of the board. The Black pawn, from its home square, has drawn abreast of the White pawn by taking a double jump. Now, to prevent the Black pawn from "passing" in this way, the White pawn is permitted to move to the square leaped over by the Black pawn, capturing just as if the Black pawn had advanced only one square. The conditions under which this *en passant* (abbreviated e.p.) capture is legal are:

(a) A White pawn (or Black) may capture e.p. a Black pawn (or White) that has just made a double jump and that it could have captured had said pawn advanced only one square.

(b) The e.p. capture is allowed only as an immediate reply to the double jump. It may not be made at any later move.

Promotion. When a pawn reaches the end of the line — the edge of the board farthest from the owner — the owner must remove it from the board and replace it with a queen, rook, bishop, or knight of his own color. This exchange is called *promotion,* or since the player usually chooses the most powerful piece, *queening.*

The rule of promotion keeps a chess game a real fight even when many of the stronger pieces are "swapped off." As long as a single pawn remains on the board, the game can end in a checkmate.

A player may acquire an additional piece by promotion even though he still has his original complement of such pieces on the board. Thus, he may have two or more queens at the same time. In a celebrated game there were at one time five queens on the board!

LAWS OF CHESS

Tournament chess is of course played under strict rules. "Social chess" is more relaxed but still must obey certain laws, which are summarized in the following paragraphs.

Illegal Moves. It is illegal to (a) move one's king onto a square guarded by an enemy piece; (b) make a move that exposes one's king to check; and (c) move a piece or pawn in a way that is outside its powers (e.g., move a knight like a bishop).

An illegal move must be retracted on demand of the opponent, and the player must then, if possible, make a legal move with the same piece. If he cannot make a legal move with the same piece, he is not penalized.

Touch Moves. A player who touches a piece or pawn in his turn to move must move it if he can do so legally.

An exception to the foregoing rule arises if a player wishes to adjust the position of his pieces; he may say "I arrange" or words to that effect and then adjust his pieces without penalty.

If, in his turn to move, a player touches an enemy piece, he must, if possible, capture it. (A player should never touch an enemy piece for the purpose of arranging; he should request his opponent to make any necessary adjustment.)

If a player moves his rook and then relinquishes it, the move is complete: he may not then move his king to complete castling. (The right way to castle is to move the king first, since the two-square jump clearly indicates the intention to castle. An alternative is to pick up the king and the rook simultaneously.)

DRAWN GAMES

A game may end in a draw in a number of ways.

Stalemate. A game is drawn if the player in turn to move has no legal move but is not in check.

Perpetual Check. A game is drawn if a player demonstrates that he can check without cessation and declares his intention to do so.

Threefold Repetition. If the same position of all forces recurs three times during a game with the same player to move each time, that player may claim a draw.

50-Move Rule. At any time a player may call upon his opponent either to give checkmate or to concede a draw within 50 moves. The count of moves begins anew whenever a pawn moves or there is a capture (i.e., whenever there is a nonretractable change in the position). The purpose of this rule is to curb a player who seeks to avoid a loss or a draw merely by prolonging the game ad infinitum.

In exceptional cases, such as two knights versus a pawn, a player is allowed to effect mate in twice the number of moves in which it is theoretically possible to do so. Thus, if the theoretical number is 60, he is allowed 120.

Insufficient Force. A game is drawn if the pieces remaining on the board, such as a lone bishop or knight, are insufficient to force checkmate.

NOTATION

The lines of squares on the chessboard are called *ranks, files,* and *diagonals.* A *rank* is a row of squares parallel to the Black and White sides of the board. A *file* is a row of squares extending from the Black to the White side.

BLACK

QR1	QN1	QB1	Q1	K1	KB1	KN1	KR1
QR8	QN8	QB8	Q8	K8	KB8	KN8	KR8
QR2	QN2	QB2	Q2	K2	KB2	KN2	KR2
QR7	QN7	QB7	Q7	K7	KB7	KN7	KR7
QR3	QN3	QB3	Q3	K3	KB3	KN3	KR3
QR6	QN6	QB6	Q6	K6	KB6	KN6	KR6
QR4	QN4	QB4	Q4	K4	KB4	KN4	KR4
QR5	QN5	QB5	Q5	K5	KB5	KN5	KR5
QR5	QN5	QB5	Q5	K5	KB5	KN5	KR5
QR4	QN4	QB4	Q4	K4	KB4	KN4	KR4
QR6	QN6	QB6	Q6	K6	KB6	KN6	KR6
QR3	QN3	QB3	Q3	K3	KB3	KN3	KR3
QR7	QN7	QB7	Q7	K7	KB7	KN7	KR7
QR2	QN2	QB2	Q2	K2	KB2	KN2	KR2
QR8	QN8	QB8	Q8	K8	KB8	KN8	KR8
QR1	QN1	QB1	Q1	K1	KB1	KN1	KR1

WHITE
I-11 Notation of the Chessboard

The files are designated according to the pieces initially posted on them: "queen's file," "king's file," etc. The left half of the board, as seen by White, is the "queen's side," and the right half is the "king's side." The designation "queen's" or "kings" is added in naming the bishops', knights', and rooks' files. In abbreviation, the files from White's left to right are: QR, QN, QB, Q, K, KB, KN, KR.

The ranks are numbered from 1 to 8. Each player numbers away from his side of the board so that each rank has a double designation: e.g., White's 4th rank is Black's 5th.

A square is designated by its rank and file, as K4, QN5, KR1. (The context must indicate whether the rank is named from the White or the Black side.) Diagram I-11 shows the names of the squares.

A noncapturing move is written by using the initial of the piece and the name of the square to which it moves, joined by a hyphen, as P-K4, which is read "pawn to king's fourth." Additional information is given if necessary to avoid ambiguity, as N-QB3 ("knight to queen's bishop's third"), R(1)-K2 ("rook on the 1st rank to king's second"). Nonessential information is suppressed: e.g., N-B3 is written instead of N-QB3 when no knight can reach KB3.

A capturing move is written by using the initials of the capturing and captured pieces, joined by the symbol "x," which is read "takes." For example, PxP is read "pawn takes pawn," and QRxBP is read "queen's rook takes bishop's pawn."

In the record of a game, each player's moves are numbered from one up. The following is the record of a brief game.

KING'S GAMBIT

WHITE	BLACK	WHITE	BLACK
1 P-K4	P-K4	4 P-N3	PxP
2 P-KB4	PxP	5 P-KR3	P-N7ch
3 P-QN3?	Q-R5ch	6 K-K2	QxKPch
		7 K-B2	PxR(N) mate

BLACK

WHITE

I-12   **Final Position**

The final position is shown in Diagram I-12. Notice that Black — quite legally — has three knights! When a pawn promotes, the piece that replaces it is inserted in parentheses after the move.

The following symbols are the ones most commonly used in chess notation:

O-O	Castles on king's side
O-O-O	Castles on queen's side
ch	Check
†	Check
‡	Checkmate
?	A bad move (read "query")
!	A good move (read "best")

The foregoing game is presented in *columnar* style. Two other styles are also encountered in chess books:

Linear: 1 P-K4, P-K4 2 P-KB4, PxP 3 P-QN3? Q-R5ch, etc.

Fractional:

	P-K4		P-KB4		P-QN3?
1	P-K4	2	PxP	3	Q-R5ch

REVIEW I

1. Who moves first in the game of chess, White or Black?
2. What is a checkmate?
3. Is it necessary to warn your opponent when you attack his king?
4. What is a stalemate?
5. What color square, light or dark, must be in the player's right-hand corner when the men are set up for play?
6. In the initial array of the chessmen, does the king or queen go on its color?
7. What do the following symbols stand for? K, Q, R, B, P, Kt, N, S, e.p.?
8. How is capture effected (with the exception of *en passant*)?
9. What is meant by the symbol O-O-O?
10. May a player, in his turn to move, touch a piece without moving it?
11. Does a knight go from a light to a light or dark square?
12. Which piece moves forward only, never backward?
13. Which piece leaps over adjoining pieces?
14. (a) How many queens is it *possible* for one side to have?
    (b) How many knights?
15. When a pawn reaches the 8th row, may it remain a pawn?

16 Can the Black king move, and if so, where?

17 White plays P-K4. May Black capture the pawn *en passant*?

18 Several moves a g o, Black played P-B4. May White now capture the pawn *en passant*?

ANSWERS TO REVIEW I

1. White.
2. A checkmate is a position with a king so attacked that he cannot possibly escape.
3. No. The warning is customary though not obligatory.
4. A stalemate is a position in which a player to move has no legal move but his king is not attacked.
5. Light.
6. The queen.

7. K for king, Q for queen, R for rook, B for bishop, P for pawn, Kt, N, and S for knight, and e.p. for *en passant*.

8. The capturing piece replaces the captured piece on the same square from which the captured piece is removed.

9. Castles on the queen's side.

10. Yes, provided that he has first said "I arrange" or words to that effect.

11. To a dark square.

12. The pawn.

13. The knight.

14. (a) Nine queens, the original one plus eight promoted ones.
(b) Ten knights, the original two and eight promoted ones.

15. No.

16. The Black king cannot move. The White pieces guard the squares around the king even though they are themselves pinned. The logic of this situation is that if the king were subject to capture, a move by Black such as K-K1 would be answered by NxK ahead of Black's reply BxK.

17. Black may not capture *en passant*. White's pawn has not made a double jump.

18. White may not capture *en passant*. The e.p. capture is allowed only as an immediate reply to the double jump: it may not be made at a later turn.

QUIZ I

1   In each of the following positions, the player whose king is at K1 has not yet moved his king or rook. May he legally castle?

1a

1b

1c

1d

2 Is this a legal position?

3 Is this a legal position?

4 Black to move, what result?

5 Black to move, what result?

6 What is Black's only move?

7 What moves may Black make?

8 White checkmates in two. How?

ANSWERS TO QUIZ I

1. (a) No. The king may not castle out of check. (b) Yes. Black may castle even though his rook is attacked. (c) Yes. White may castle even though his rook passes over a square attacked by an enemy piece. (d) No. Black may not castle when his king must pass over a square attacked by an enemy piece.

2. The position is not legal. A king may not move to a square commanded by an enemy piece; hence, the two kings can never approach each other so as to stand adjacent.

3. The position is not legal. Both kings are in check—an impossibility since the player who moved last must either have left his king in check or moved him into check.

4. Black is checkmated. He is attacked by the queen, who also guards the adjacent dark squares, and he cannot capture the queen, for she is guarded by the White king.

5. Black has no legal move but is not in check. This is a stalemate —a draw.

6. The Black king is in check. The only legal way to meet the check is to move the queen right across the board, interposing on the line of the rook. (Then the rook can capture the queen, checkmating.)

7. Black must avert the check from the queen. He has three options:
   (a)   To move the king to KN8.
   (b)   To interpose the bishop at KR7.
   (c)   To capture the queen with his knight.

8. 1 Q-N4ch, K-K4   2 Q-K4
              , K-K2   2 BxP
              , K-Q4   2 Q-K4
              , P-B4   2 PxP e.p.

The main point of the problem, composed by the famous composer of chess problems, Sam Loyd, is the last variation. With one fell *en passant* capture, White cuts off innumerable avenues of escape for the Black king and delivers checkmate.

Lesson II

BASIC CHECKMATES

The object of chess is to checkmate your opponent's king. After "the moves" the next thing to learn is how to force checkmate with the minimum number of pieces. The endings we will discuss first almost never arise in actual play, because the weaker side usually resigns when faced with sure loss. Nevertheless, you must know the principles of these endings. They may arise even when both sides have equal pieces but the weaker side cannot bring his pieces to the defense of his king.

MATE WITH ROOK

Diagram II-1 shows the only possible positions in which a Black king can be mated by a lone White rook. At the lower right, the

II-1   **Rook Mates**

Black king stands on the edge of the board, the White king is directly opposed, and the rook checks along the edge. In general, this mate cannot be forced easily, for the Black king runs away from the direct opposition of the White king. It is usually necessary to drive the

Black king into a corner, as shown at the upper left. The White king can then stand on either of two squares (QN6 or QR6).

Now let us consider how to drive the lone king to the edge of the board and then to a corner. Wherever the White rook stands, it confines the Black king to a square or rectangle smaller than the board itself, as shown in Diagram II-2. The Black king cannot pass across the K-file nor downward across White's 4th rank. The process of driving the king back consists of advancing the rook toward the king at every opportunity so as to make the rectangle smaller.

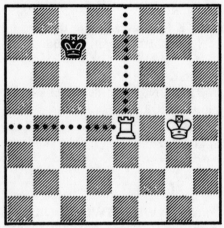

II-2   The Rook's Rectangle

To check the king at any time before the final checkmate is usually a mistake. In Diagram II-2, if White begins by 1 R-B4ch, the king goes toward the K-side, thus stepping from a smaller rectangle into a larger one. A check is therefore a forward step for White only if his king stands near enough to prevent the Black king from escaping into the larger area.

Since the Black king can approach the White rook diagonally and threaten to capture it, White must bring his king up to guard the rook. Even then, he could not advance the rook effectively were it not for *Zugzwang*—the compulsion to move. If the Black king could stay on the square diagonally adjacent to the rook, White could make no headway. But the rules compel Black to move in his regular turn. Thus he must step away from the rook, which can then advance if the White king is near enough to guard it.

In Diagram II-2 the play might go:

1 R-K6

Cutting the rectangle in half.

1 . . .   K-Q2
2 K-B5

If the White king stood more distant, White would first move his rook away from the attack, say to KR6, then bring his king up.

2 . . .   K-B2
3 K-K5   K-Q2
4 K-Q5

Not 4 R-Q6ch, K-K2, escaping into the larger rectangle.

4 . . .   K-B2   6 R-B6   K-N1
5 R-Q6   K-N2   7 K-B5   K-N2
               8 K-N5   K-R1

Or 8 . . . K-R2 9 R-N6, then the White king moves to B6 and B7, and the rook mates on QR-file.

9 K-N6   K-N1
10 R-B1

A waiting move.

10 . . .   K-R1
11 R-B8 mate

MATE WITH TWO ROOKS

With two rooks against a lone king, you could, of course, leave one of them behind and mate with the other. But it is important

II-3   **Mate with Two Rooks**

to note that two rooks can mate without help from their king. The process is a "creeping barrage." In Diagram II-3 the play might go:

1	R-KR4		K-B4
2	R-QR5ch		K-N3
3	R-KN5		

Moving away from the king's attack. Not 3 QR-KR5, because that would interfere with the other rook.

3 . . .	K-B3	5 R-N7ch	K-K1
4 R-R6ch	K-Q2	6 R-R8 mate	

MATE WITH TWO BISHOPS

To mate with two bishops, a player must drive the lone king into a corner. The principle of driving him back is based on the fact that, when the bishops stand on adjacent diagonals, they create a diagonal barrier across the board and thus confine the enemy king to a triangular space. With the help of their king, the bishops advance their barrier toward the enemy king and thus decrease the triangle.

II-4   **Mate with Two Bishops**

From Diagram II-4 the play might go:

1	K-Q3	K-B4
2	B-B3	

The bishops must hem in the enemy by erecting a barrier in the other direction.

2 . . .	K-N4
3 B-B2	K-B4
4 B-N3	

Seizing the opportunity to decrease the original triangle.

4 . . .	K-N4	7 B-R3	K-B3
5 K-Q4	K-B3	8 B-B4	K-N3
6 B-N4	K-N4	9 B-N4	K-B3
10 K-K5			

Since the Black king has no avenue of approach to attack the bishops, the White king can leave them in order to help the drive.

| 10 . . . | K-Q2 |
| 11 B-N5ch | |

This check is feasible because the White king prevents the enemy's escape through the diagonal that the bishop has forsaken: e.g., 11 . . . K-Q1 12 K-K6.

| 11 . . . | K-B2 | 13 B-R4 | K-B2 |
| 12 K-K6 | K-N3 | 14 B-R5ch | |

Again a feasible check, because the bishop can leave his diagonal without letting the enemy escape.

14 . . .	K-B1	16 B-N5	K-B1
15 K-Q6	K-N2	17 K-B6	K-N1
18 B-B1			

The bishops must now about-face so as to operate on the diagonals from lower right to upper left.

18 . . .	K-R2	20 B-K1	K-R2
19 K-B7	K-R1	21 B-B2ch	K-R1
22 B-N2 mate			

MATE WITH QUEEN

Since the queen has the powers of a rook, she can force checkmate as a rook. The "sideboard" mate is easier, however, since the friendly king need not stand directly opposed to the enemy (right edge of Diagram II-5). But the queen's possession of bishop powers enables her to deliver mates not possible with the rook, as shown at the top and bottom of Diagram II-5.

II-5   **Queen Mates**

Since the Black king cannot approach the White queen, he can be driven into a corner without help of the White king, but the White king must be brought up to do guard duty in the mate. We shall not illustrate this easy process, but we give warning to beware of an inadvertent stalemate. The chief danger arises from the position in which the Black king has been cornered and the White queen stands a knight-move away (Diagram II-6). With Black to move,

II-6   **Stalemate Pitfalls**

this is a stalemate and a draw wherever the White king stands. A side-board stalemate is shown in the lower part of the diagram. The moral of these positions is: at all times before the final blow, be sure that you leave the Black king a move!

MATE WITH A BISHOP AND KNIGHT

This mate is long and difficult. It will not be given in full, but we will point out some principles. The ideal position of the

II-7   The Bishop-Knight Barrier

pieces to erect a barrier against the lone king is shown in Diagram II-7. The two pieces stand on the same rank, two squares apart. The bishop guards squares of one color, and the knight guards squares of the other. This barrier necessarily dissolves when the pieces advance, for the knight changes color with every move. Therefore the friendly king must be extremely active in assisting his pieces.

The Black king must be driven into the corner *of the same color as the bishop,* or, in the diagram, White's QR8 or KR1. The Black king will naturally retreat, when forced, into the wrong corner, whence he must be driven along the side of the board to the right corner.

II-8   **Bishop-Knight Mate**

The final position must be essentially that shown in Diagram II-8. White plays 1 N-B8ch, K-R1 2 B-N2 mate. The mate must be given by the bishop: it cannot be forced with the knight.

INSUFFICIENT FORCE

A single minor piece, bishop or knight, cannot give checkmate, since no mate position can be set up. A mate can be set up with two knights against the lone king, but it cannot be forced. Diagram II-9

II-9 The Two Knights Cannot Mate

shows the reason. The Black king has been cornered, and the knights stand as favorably as they can. White may move 1 N-B6ch, K-R1, but now the other knight, already on a dark square, cannot in one move reach another dark square (QB7) to give mate. There is no time for 2 N-K8 with intention of 3 N-B7 mate, for Black is stalemated.

Mate with Two Knights. White can sometimes mate with two knights if Black has a pawn, for then the possibility of moving

II-10 The Two Knights Can Mate

the pawn averts the stalemate. Diagram II-10 shows an actual game. White has carefully refrained from capturing the Black pawn and has delegated one knight to block it. With the other knight and the king he has driven the enemy into a corner (a possible but difficult process). Now he plays:

| 1 N-Q4 | P-K7 | 3 N-K8 | P queens |
| 2 N-B6ch | K-R1 | 4 N-B7 mate | |

Mate with One Minor Piece. The presence of officious friends may betray the Black king and admit a mate by a single minor White piece. To illustrate, here are two famous problems. In Diagram II-11 the play goes:

II-11   **White Mates in Five**

1 N-B6	K-R8
2 N-K4	K-R7

Not 2 . . . P-R7 3 N-N3 mate.

3 N-Q2	K-R8
4 N-B1	P-R7
5 N-N3 mate	

II-12   **White Mates in Four**

In Diagram II-12 the play goes:

1 P queens, ch	KxQ
2 K-K6!	

Insufficient Force •

2 KxP leaves a drawn game.

2 . . .	K-R1
3 K-B7	P moves
4 B-N7 mate	

QUEEN VERSUS ROOK

The general position of this ending is shown in Diagram II-13. The Black rook must stay under the guard of its king; otherwise

II-13   **Queen versus Rook in General Position**

it may be lost through a queen check that attacks both Black pieces simultaneously. The White king must come as close to his opponent as possible to aid the queen in driving him back. The White forces triumph. If Black is to move, the play may be:

1 . . .	K-B2

Not K-K2, for then 2 K-K5 and wins the rook.

2 K-Q5	R-N3
3 Q-B5ch	R-B3

If K-N2, 3 K-K5 and White has achieved his purpose in driving the enemy nearer the corner.

4 Q-R7ch	K-B1	6 Q-R8ch	K-K2
5 K-K5	R-B2	7 Q-QB8	

The Black king has been forced back one rank and the White queen has reached the ideal post.

When the Black king is finally forced to the edge, White must proceed a little differently to avoid a stalemate. Suppose that Black is to move in Diagram II-14.

II-14   Beware Stalemate

| 1 . . . | K-K1 |
| 2 K-B6? | R-B2ch! |

If 3 KxR, the game is a draw by stalemate.

| 3 K-Q6?? | R-B3ch! |

Now White must capture the rook or lose his Queen, and Black obtains the draw.

The correct continuation is:

| 1 . . . | K-K1 |
| 2 Q-B5 | |

By guarding his Q7, White prevents the return of the Black king and also lets his own king advance without being checked away.

2 . . .	R-Q2ch
3 K-B6	R-K2
4 K-Q6	R-KN2

Not R-KB2 5 Q-B8 mate. If the rook goes elsewhere, White wins it eventually by a forking check.

5 Q-R5ch	K-B1
6 K-K6	R-K2ch
7 K-B6	

And White soon mates.

If in Diagram II-14 it is White's turn to move, he must beware of the following lines:

| 1 Q-B6ch | K-Q1 |
| 2 K-Q6?? | R-K3ch! |

or

| 1 Q-QN6 | K-B1! |

Again the White king cannot advance because of the rook check at K3.

| 2 Q-B6ch | K-Q1 |
| 3 Q-Q6ch?? | R-Q2 |

Another variant is 3 K-B5? R-QB2.

The right continuation for White from II-14 is:

| 1 Q-B8 | R-K1 |

Black has no other move unless he wants to send his rook "into left field."

| 2 Q-Q6ch | K-B1 |
| 3 K-B6 | |

And mates soon.

We have remarked that, if the Black rook runs away, attempting to check the White king from the rear, it is likely to be lost. However, White is under no compulsion to work out the sometimes intricate geometry of this process: he can rest content to drive the Black king back while protecting himself from disruptive checks. For example, suppose that from II-14 the play goes:

| 1 Q-B8 | R-K8 |

II-15   The Rook Runs Away

2 Q-B3

The rook is now compelled to return to K2, and the winning process is that already outlined. If the rook persists in remaining far afield, it is bound to be lost. To cover every conceivable rook move is beyond the scope of the paragraph. We will, however, assume that the rook goes to KN8.

2 . . .   R-KN8

3 Q-B5ch

By the correct series of moves, White will deliver a connecting check that will fork king and rook.

3 . . .   K-K1

4 Q-QB8ch   K-B2

5 Q-B7ch   K-N1

If 5 . . . K-B3 or 5 . . . K-N3, 6 Q-N6ch forks king and rook.

6 Q-N8ch!

Wherever Black plays, the rook is lost.

6 . . .   K-R2

If 6 . . . K-N2, 7 Q-R7ch forks king and rook.

7 Q-R2ch

The rook falls.

II-16　　Getting past the Rook

The position of II-16 is important for theory, because the inexperienced player is often not sure how to continue. The idea is to get the king into action by a tour.

1 K-K8	R-B1ch		

Or R-B3 2 Q-R5!

2 K-K7	R-B2ch	4 K-K5	R-N3
3 K-K6	R-B3ch	5 Q-R5	R-KR3
6 Q-N5ch	R-N3		

Now, for lack of space, White must proceed differently from the line given above.

7 Q-K7ch	K-R3	10 Q-R5	R-B1ch
8 K-B5	R-N1	11 K-K6	R-B3ch
9 Q-R4ch	K-N2	12 K-K7	R-N3
13 Q-R4	K-N1		

Or R-R3 14 Q-N4ch, R-N3 15 Q-R5, and White, having changed "the move," wins as in II-14.

| 14 Q-Q4 | K-R2 |
| 15 K-B7 | |

And mates soon.

ROOK VERSUS BISHOP

This is a draw, but the weaker side must play carefully. The chief point to remember is that, if your king (you being the weaker party) is forced to the edge of the board, post him on a square

II-17 Rook versus Bishop

of the same color as your bishop. Consider Diagram II-17, Black to move. (If it is White's turn, he waits with R-N7.) The plausible error is 1 . . . K-K1, with the idea of retaining the chance to interpose the bishop on a check. But then 2 K-K6, B-R6 3 R-R8ch, B-B1 4 R-N8, and the bishop is lost. The right move is 1 . . . K-Q1. The bishop prevents the enemy king from taking the square of *direct opposition* (Q6), wherefore a rook check can never be a mate. (For *direct opposition* see Lesson III.)

ROOK VERSUS KNIGHT

This is a draw, relatively easy for the weaker party to play. Even if his king is forced to the edge, as in Diagram II-18, the

II-18   Rook versus Knight

adjacent knight, interposed on a rook check, prevents the enemy king from taking the square of direct opposition (Q6). The Black king threatens to escape via K2. If White moves 1 R-R7, Black can move either 1 . . . N-B3 or K-B1 without danger. Almost the only trap to avoid is the position of II-18 with the White king on K6 instead of QB6; here the knight is lost.

OTHER PAWNLESS ENDINGS

Queen versus two rooks is a draw, provided that one player does not lose immediately through the awkward placement of his pieces. Queen versus three minor pieces is a draw. Two bishops usually draw easily against a queen, but a bishop and a knight or two knights usually lose. Queen versus one minor piece is an easy win, because the weaker side is unable to prevent the rapid approach of both the queen and the king. In other pawnless endings, the rule is that a player wins if his preponderance of pieces is in itself a mating force; e.g., a rook accompanied by a knight or bishop wins against a single minor piece. To summarize:

White has	Black has	Result
Q	. . .	White wins
Q	R, B, or N	White wins
Q	N+N	White wins
Q	B+N	White usually wins
Q	B+B	Usually drawn
Q	R+ (R, B, or N)	Draw
R	. . .	White wins
R	B or N	Draw
B+B	. . .	White wins
B+N	. . .	White wins
N+N	. . .	Draw
B or N	. . .	Draw

RELATIVE VALUE OF THE PIECES

In chess, any *material inferiority* (fewer pieces or less total force than the opponent) spells potential defeat. How often we read the annotation, "White wins a pawn; the rest is merely a matter of technique." Of course, circumstances alter cases. Positions can arise in which a knight is worth more than a queen. Material inferiority is often tolerable because it is offset by *positional superiority*. But these exceptions are more apparent than real. You should sacrifice or submit to loss of force only if you see your way clear to effecting checkmate or to capturing enough enemy pieces to restore equality.

To estimate the material situation, count the number of pieces of each kind on both sides. Thus, you may say mentally, "I have six pawns, and so has my opponent. I have a queen, and so has he . . ." Often, the two armies can be set into one-to-one correspondence. At other times, a few unlike pieces are left over, such as a rook on one side against a bishop and pawn on the other. To complete the estimate, you must know the relative values of the pieces.

Numerical Values. From the basic endings you probably already have a good idea of these relative values. Other factors are the total number of squares each piece can command and the verdict of experience. When all factors are taken together, it is found that the relative values, in terms of the pawn as 1, are:

Queen	9
Rook	5
Bishop	3
Knight	3
Pawn	1

The king is, of course, invaluable, but in terms of this scale his fighting power is about 5.

Winning the Exchange. White and Black begin a game with equal forces. The balance can be disrupted only by captures. You must remember these relative values particularly when an *exchange* (capture and return capture) of pieces is in prospect. A player is said to *win the exchange* when he captures greater force at the cost of lesser. The most common examples are the capture of an enemy rook for a bishop or knight and the capture of two minor pieces for a rook.

TABLE FOR EXCHANGES

(Read $=$ "is equal to." Read $>$ "is worth more than.")

Q(+P)* $=$ R+R	B+N $>$ R
Q $>$ R+ (B or N)	B+N $=$ R+P
Q $=$ B+N+ (B or N)	B or N $=$ P+P+P
R+B+N $>$ Q	R$>$ B or N
B $=$ N	R$=$ P+P+ (B or N)

REVIEW II

1. Can a queen force mate in the center of the board when no other pieces but the kings are present?
2. Can two knights force mate?
3. With no other pieces left, can a queen win against a rook?
4. What does *Zugzwang* mean?
5. Can a bishop and a knight force checkmate?
6. How many pawns are considered equivalent to a bishop?
7. Can a rook win against (a) a bishop? (b) a knight?
8. In what two ways can the presence of a Black pawn be harmful to Black when White has only two knights?

---

*The (+P) is inserted to balance the equation. But this exchange, more than any other, depends on the position of the other forces. The "heavy pieces" have great potential power to capitalize on a momentary weakness of the enemy position.

9. Is a rook worth more or less than two knights?

10. The queen and rook are called *major* pieces; the bishop and knight are called *minor*. What is the essential difference between the major and minor pieces?

ANSWERS TO REVIEW II

1. No, the enemy king can be mated only at the edge of the board or in a corner.

2. No.

3. Yes, in general. The rook can draw (usually by stalemate) only if the enemy makes a mistake.

4. The compulsion to move. A player is said to be in *Zugzwang* when he cannot hold a defensible position intact: any move he makes is bound to impair it.

5. Yes. This is one of the most difficult endings.

6. Three.

7. (a) No. (b) No.

8. The Black pawn may enable White to mate because (a) it lifts the stalemate, which is otherwise the most that the knights can achieve, or (b) it blocks a square to which the Black king could otherwise escape.

9. Less, by about the value of a pawn.

10. A single major piece (with help from its king) can force mate; a single minor piece cannot.

QUIZ II

1   Judge the following endings in terms of "W wins" or "B wins" or "Draw." (Besides the given pieces, only the kings are on the board. All pieces are adequately protected, and the kings are safe from sudden mating attacks.)

	W has	*B has*	*Result*
(a)	R,R	R,N	. . . .
(b)	Q,R	B,B,N	. . . .
(c)	N,N	R,B	. . . .
(d)	R,B	Q,N	. . . .
(e)	Q,B	R,R	. . . .
(f)	R,R	B,B,N	. . . .
(g)	R,B,N	Q	. . . .

2 What is White's best move?

3 What is White's best move?

4 What White move leads to the quickest mate?

5 Show how White can win the rook.

6 What is the simplest winning process f o r White?

7 White to move and mate. How?

8 The player to move wins. How?

9 White draws. How?

10 Show how White mates in 3.

11 White mates in 7. How?

12 White to move. Can Black win?

13 White can win. How?

14 White mates. How?

15 White mates in 4. How?

16 White to move and win. How?

17 White mates in 5. How?

18 This is a crucial position of the B and N ending. Can you find the way White can play to crowd the Black king into the corner?

ANSWERS TO QUIZ II

1. (a) Draw. In general, these positions can be simplified by considering the ending after like or equal pieces on both sides have been exchanged. Here, after an exchange of rooks, the R versus N is a draw. (b) W wins (barring exceptional cases). At worst, W can choose his own time to give up his rook for a bishop, reducing the game to a position in which the queen can win against bishop and knight. (c) Draw. (d) B wins. (e) W wins, in general, by winning a rook for his bishop. But in some positions W can make no headway because his own king is bothered by checks. The win is much easier with some pawns on the board, so that the White king can find shelter. (f) Draw. (g) Draw, but W has all the chances. B can usually threaten perpetual check or the win of a piece if the W pieces go away from their king in an effort to weave a mating net. With some pawns on the board, W can often win.

2. Not K-N2 or K-N3! That would stalemate. Best is 1 Q-B2, K-B8 2 Q-Q2, K-N8 3 Q-K1 or Q-KN2 mate.

3. R-B7ch. Exceptionally, this check does not let the king step into a larger rectangle but forces him back.

4. Q-Q7. Hold the Black king as near the White king as possible, to shorten the latter's trek. (There is mate in 7, e.g., 1 Q-Q7, K-B3 2 K-B2, K-K4 3 K-B3, K-B3 4 K-B4, K-N3 5 Q-K7, K-R3 6 K-B5, K-R4 7 Q-R7 or N5 mate.)

5. 1 Q-Q8ch, K-R2 2 Q-K7ch, K-N1 3 Q-B8ch, K-R2 4 Q-B7ch, K-N1 5 Q-N8ch, K-R2 6 Q-R2ch and 7 QxR. By similar play White can win the rook if it runs away from the QN2 to another square.

6. White wins quickly if Black has to move from this position (e.g., 1 . . . K-B1 2 Q-R6 or 1 . . . R-QR2 2 Q-Q8 mate). The simplest course is to reproduce it with Black to move, by "triangulation": 1 Q-K5ch, K-R2 or R1, 2 Q-R1ch, K-N1 3 Q-R5.

7. 1 QxRch! RxQ 2 R-K8ch, RxR 3 RxR mate. This illustrates the danger of failing to give the king an outlet (as by P-KR3) after castling, when the enemy heavy pieces (rooks and queen) are in action.

8. White wins by Q-K4ch, capturing the advanced rook. Black wins by 1 . . . RxPch! 2 K or QxR, R-N3, pinning the queen and

then winning her. Black emerges with four pawns against three, enough to win.

9. 1 Q-K8ch, K-N2 2 Q-K7ch, K-R3 3 Q-R4ch, K-N2 4 Q-K7ch, and can claim a draw by perpetual check.

10. Any waiting move with the rook will do, as 1 R-K1. Then 1 ... K-B1 is answered by 2 R-KN1 and 1 ... K-Q1 by 2 R-QB1. In either case the Black king must return to K1, and then the rook on the 8th rank mates.

11. 1 R-N1, K-R5 (if K-R7 2 R-N3 and mates next) 2 K-B3, K-R4 (if the Black king moves the other way, he walks into opposition and the rook mates at once) 3 K-B4, K-R3 4 K-B5, K-R2 5 K-B6, K-R1 6 K-B7, K-R2 7 R-R1 mate.

12. No! This position is the one exception to the rule that the queen wins against the rook. White checks at KN2, KR2, and KB2. The Black king cannot get out of the checks by going to the K-file, for then R-K2 pins the queen and captures her. Nor does the Black king escape by going to KR6, for then R-R2ch, and KxR is useless because of a stalemate. If the king goes to KB6 to prevent R-B2ch, then R-N3ch forces KxR, stalemate. Thus Black can escape perpetual check only by conceding the draw in another way. Observe that this exceptional position arises only because the edge of the board prevents the Black king from stepping one file to the right of KR-file to escape the checks. (Black to move could of course win, most directly by 1 ... Q-K5.)

13. White can capture the knight: 1 R-B6 to command the squares (White's) QN6 and QB5. Now White threatens K-B2-N3 then xN. If 1 ... N-N7ch, 2 K-B2, and the knight is forced right back to R5. This position illustrates the fact that a rook can sometimes win against a knight if the knight wanders too far away from the protection of his king.

14. 1 Q-R6ch, K-B2 2 R-B8ch, K-K2 3 Q-B6ch, K-Q2 4 R-Q8ch, K-B2 5 Q-Q6ch, K-N2 6 R-N8ch, K-R2 7 Q-N6 mate. It is useful to know this process.

15. 1 B-R3, K-R8 2 K-N3, K-N8 3 B-Q3ch, K-R8 4 B-N2 mate.

16. 1 R-R4. The bishop must maintain guard of his KR1 to prevent mate. If he goes to B6, N7, or R8, the rook attacks him on the file, simultaneously threatening mate, and the bishop is therefore lost. The only other move is 1 ... B-N2. Then 2 R-QR4

threatens mate and 2 . . . K-B1 is no defense because the bishop
blocks the king's outlet. If 2 . . . K-Q1, then 3 R-R8ch, and
4 R-R7ch wins the bishop. This is but one of the many positions
in which Black can lose by letting his king be forced to the edge
of the board with the White king in direct opposition.

17. There are several ways. One way is 1 B-Q8, K-N1 2 B-K7,
K-R1 3 N-B5, K-N1 4 N-R6ch, K-R1 5 B-B6 mate.

18. Do not be dismayed if you failed to find the answer. This difficult ending is given for the purpose of instruction. The line
is: 1 N-R5ch (an unlikely-looking move, but the N must get
out of the way of his own king) K-N3 (best) 2 N-N3, K-N2
3 B-N5, K-N3 4 B-B6! K-R2 5 K-B7. The rest is easy: 5 . . .
K-R3 6 B-K8, K-R2 7 B-N5, K-R1 8 B-R6, K-R2 9 B-B8, K-R1
10 N-R5, K-R2 11 N-B6ch, K-R1 12 B-N7 mate.

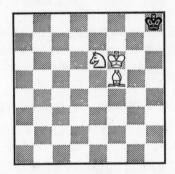

The position of No. 18 can arise from the diagram shown, in
which the Black king has fled to the "wrong corner," as follows:
1 N-Q8, K-N1 2 N-B7, K-B1 3 B-R7, K-K1 4 N-K5. If Black
now tries to stay on the K-side with 4 . . . K-B1, the continuation
is 5 N-Q7ch, K-K1 6 K-K6, K-Q1 7 K-Q6, K-K1 8 B-N6ch,
K-Q1 9 N-B5, etc. Black would do better to rush quickly to the
Q-side while the pieces are still on the other side: 4 . . . K-Q1
5 K-K6, K-B2 6 B-B2! K-N3 7 K-Q5, K-N4 8 N-B6, K-N3 9
K-Q6, K-N4 10 B-N3, K-N3 11 B-B4, K-N2 (No. 18). Observe
how the White pieces have swung to the Q-side just in time to
prevent the Black king from escaping to the lower left corner.

Lesson III

PAWN ENDINGS

This lesson is a continuation of Lesson II on basic endings. Now, however, we turn to endings with pawns on the board. This addition often radically changes the evaluation of the ending and of the objectives of play. The fighting power of the pawn is small, but its potential power is enormous. Pawn endings are characterized by the aim to realize this potential, i.e., to queen a pawn.

In the Table of Pawnless Endings (see page 37) the endings marked as "White wins" may be little affected by the presence of pawns. White's preponderance is such that he can usually head straight for checkmate without bothering to queen a pawn. But the endings noted as draws become wins for White if equal pawns are added on both sides, because White's preponderance in fighting force enables him to win the battle of queening.

THE SQUARE OF QUEENING

In Diagram III-1, the White pawn can queen in four moves. To catch it, the Black king must make five moves (to his KN1).

III-1   The Square of Queening

Therefore, if it is White's turn to move, he wins the race, but if it is Black's turn he can head for KN1 and arrive just in time.

The question of whether the enemy king can catch a passed pawn is thus merely a matter of counting moves. But counting is often made unnecessary by resort to the concept of the *square of queening.**

The square on which the pawn stands (KN4) and that on which it would queen (KN8) define one side of a large square. Picture this large square mentally, as shown by the dotted lines in III-1. If the king stands anywhere within this *square of queening* at the time the pawn begins to advance, then the king can catch the pawn.

III-2   The Fatal Obstruction

The foregoing rule assumes, however, that the king has clear passage. In Diagram III-2, Black loses even when it is his turn to move. He can step into the square of queening by K-B5, but the White pawn goes on, and the Black king finds his route to his KN1 obstructed by his own pawn. (If Black plays 1 . . . P-K4 and goes after a queen of his own, the White pawn queens first *with a check,* after which White can win the Black pawn.)

---

*Usually called the "queening square," but this term is ambiguous, since it also denotes the square (KN8) on which the pawn queens.

Diagram III-3 is the general position of king and pawn versus lone king. The crucial question is: Can White force his pawn past

III-3   **One-Pawn Ending**

the enemy king and queen it? The answer involves the larger question of *the opposition*, which we shall introduce by showing two possible lines of play without annotation.

One possible line is:

1	P-K4	K-K2
2	K-K2	K-K3
3	K-K3	K-K4
4	K-Q3	K-K3
5	K-Q4	K-Q3
6	P-K5ch	K-K3
7	K-K4	K-K2
8	K-Q5	K-Q2
9	P-K6ch	K-K2
10	K-K5	K-K1
11	K-Q6	K-Q1
12	P-K7ch	K-K1

III-4   White to Move: Draw

Thus we reach Diagram III-4. If White moves 12 K-K6, Black is stalemated. After any other White move, Black captures the pawn. In either case the upshot is a draw.

Beginning again from Diagram III-3, White may instead play:

1	K-Q2	K-K2
2	K-K3	K-K3
3	K-K4	K-Q3
4	K-B5	K-Q2
5	P-K4	K-K2
6	K-K5	K-Q2
7	K-B6	K-K1
8	P-K5	K-Q2
9	K-B7	

III-5   **White Wins**

Thus we reach Diagram III-5. White has driven the Black king off the K-file, and now his pawn is free to march right down.

THE OPPOSITION

You will notice that in the winning process above White opposed his king to Black's and by *Zugzwang* forced the enemy to step aside. We can say flatly that the one-pawn ending can be won only if the friendly king can *gain the opposition* while standing in front of the pawn. The factor of the opposition is decisive in many end games.

III-6   **Direct and Diagonal Opposition**

The pairs of kings at the upper left and right of Diagram III-6 illustrate *direct opposition*; the adversaries stand on the same file or rank, with one square intervening. The player who has to move from such a position finds "the opposition" (or what in checkers is called "the move") *against him,* for he cannot prevent the enemy from advancing. Thus, Black to move cannot prevent the White king at QN5 from reaching the 8th rank: 1 . . . K-B2 2 K-R6, K-N1 3 K-N6, K-B1 4 K-R7.

The pair of kings at the lower right of III-6 illustrates *diagonal opposition.* Again, the player to move is at a disadvantage; he cannot prevent the enemy from passing him in one direction or the other. After 1 . . . K-N7 2 K-K2 or 1 . . . K-B8 2 K-B3, White holds the direct opposition.

When the kings stand far apart, which will win the opposition if they race toward each other? The answer may be found by counting moves, or by applying the simple rule of the *distant opposition* (provided that no obstacles intervene). Count the number of files or ranks (whichever is greater) between the kings; the player to move holds the opposition when this number is *even* and has the opposition against him when the number is *odd.*

III-7   **Distant Opposition**

In Diagram III-7 the kings are separated by six ranks. The player to move therefore holds the opposition. White to move can go all the way to the 8th rank, e.g., 1 K-K2, K-K2 2 K-K3, K-Q3

3 K-Q4, K-K3 4 K-B5, etc. Black to move can prevent White from getting past his own 3rd rank, e.g., 1 . . . K-K2 2 K-Q2, K-Q3 3 K-K3, K-K4 4 K-B3, K-B4, etc.

You cannot use the opposition to penetrate and still retain it (by king moves alone). Returning to III-6, upper left, we see that after 1 . . . K-B2 2 K-R6, K-B3 Black has gained the opposition. White can reach KR8, if that is his purpose, but Black now can prevent him from getting off the KR-file. However, there must be pieces on the board besides the kings, and moves by these pieces often have a voice in the gain or loss of the opposition.

ONE-PAWN ENDING (Continued)

III-8   Changing the Opposition

An important instance of what was said above is illustrated in Diagram III-8. White to move has the opposition against him. Were his pawn on K4 the game would be drawn. Happily for him, he can make a temporizing move with the pawn, whereby he wrests the opposition from Black and wins. In pawn endings without other pieces, the hoarding and wise expenditure of such "reserve moves" often decide the issue.

III-9 Either to Move: White Wins

Diagram III-9 shows a position useful to remember. With this constellation of pieces, however high or low on the board and whichever is to move, White wins. If 1 . . . K-K2, 2 K-K5 takes the opposition. If 1 . . . K-B2, 2 K-Q6. Or, White moving first, 1 K-Q6, K-B2 2 P-K5, and the constellation has moved up a rank.

III-10   White to Move Wins
Black to Move Draws

Diagram III-10 is cited to clarify the play of III-3. Even the wrong line will win if Black erroneously lets this position arise with White to move, for 1 P-K7, K-B2 2 K-Q7, and the pawn queens.

The point for Black to remember is: when finally forced to the back row, he should move straight back from the pawn, staying on the same file. The White king has to step aside from his pawn to advance, then move onto the same file, and take the opposition.

The Rook's Pawn. A pawn on the R-file is an exception to the general rule. It cannot be queened even though its king gains

III-11 The RP Cannot Be Queened

the opposition in front of it. The upper left of Diagram III-11 shows the most favorable position White can obtain with Black to move. But after 1 . . . K-N1 the White king's "passing move" (to left and upward) is checked by the edge of the board. Black can forever shuttle between N1 and R1.

Furthermore, the RP cannot be queened even if the enemy king is excluded from its file, provided that the latter can reach his B1 or B2 on that wing before the pawn has reached its 7th rank. See lower right of III-11. Black to move can shut the enemy out of the corner by 1 . . . K-R7. But then 2 K-B2, P-R6 3 K-B1, and how can the pawn get by? If 3 . . . K-N6, 4 K-N1 and gets into the corner. If 3 . . . K-R8 followed by advancing the pawn, Black stalemates himself, since the White king shuttles forever between B1 and B2.

III-12   **White to Draw**

An instructive exercise in counting is Diagram III-12. Black can cross over and capture the White pawn. Whether White can draw depends on whether he can reach his KB2 in time. At the moment, White has only two moves, and the natural inclination is 1 K-B8, going "nearer" the pawns. Then 1 . . . K-B3 2 K-Q8, K-Q4, and Black wins the race, as you should verify. Strange to say, the "going away" move 1 K-R8 draws. For then 1 . . . K-B4 (useless is K-B2 2 K-R7) 2 K-N7 and White arrives in time. You will do well to figure out the reason for this anomaly before reading the explanation as follows:

> All squares on White's 8th rank are equidistant (6 moves) from his KB2. Therefore any square on the 8th is as good as another, as long as the king is hemmed in. The Black king initially stands 6 moves from the White pawn. In moving 1 . . . K-B3, Black decreases this distance to 5, because the greater dimension of the rectangle in which he stands with the pawn is *lateral*; hence the lateral move toward the pawn is a genuine approach. It is vital for White to shorten his own path when Black shortens his, and White can achieve this only by stepping away from the opposition of the Black king.

QUEEN VERSUS PAWN

As an introduction to the study of endings with pawns on both sides, we will take up the queen-versus-pawn ending. This seems like a very unequal struggle, and indeed it is if the pawn is not far advanced. The queen merely settles on the pawn's queening square, blockading it and fending off the enemy king. Then the friendly king comes up and aids in capturing the pawn. But the ending may arise from a situation in which both players have passed pawns, and both queen. The player who queens first gains an obvious advantage thereby. The question is: does this advantage suffice for a win? On the answer depend decisions that must be made in the fight of pawns versus pawns.

III-13   **Queen versus Pawn:**
General Position

The general position is shown in Diagram III-13; White has made a new queen, and it is his turn to move when the Black pawn has reached the 7th rank; the Black king guards the pawn and keeps the queen from occupying the queening square (Q8). White can win this position: 1 Q-B4ch, K-N7 2 Q-Q3, K-B8 3 Q-B3ch, K-Q8. The Black king can always be forced in front of his pawn, and thus White gains a *tempo* to bring his own king nearer. White repeats the process until the White king is near enough to co-operate in winning the pawn or in mating. For example, suppose that the White king stands on KB4 (instead of KB6). Then, after the given moves, 4 K-K3, K-K8 5 QxPch, K-B1 6 Q-B2 mate. Or, suppose that the White king stands on KN1; then 4 Q-B4, K-K8 5 Q-KB1 mate.

Rook's Pawn. We find another exception involving the pawn on the R-file in Diagram III-14. Suppose that White tries the

III-14   **Drawn Game**

process, 1 Q-N4ch, K-B7 2 Q-R3, K-N8 3 Q-N3ch, K-R8. Now White cannot utilize the tempo to bring his king up, because Black is stalemated. White cannot win this ending unless his king is already close enough to aid in mating. (Put the king on K4, and White wins by 1 Q-B3ch, K-N8 2 K-K3, P queens 3 Q-B2 mate.)

The Bishop's Pawn. A pawn on the B-file is likewise an exception. In Diagram III-15, try 1 Q-N4ch, K-R7 2 Q-B3, K-N8

III-15   **Drawn Game**

3 Q-N3ch. Now Black is under no compulsion to protect his pawn; he should move 3 . . . K-R8, for then 4 QxP produces stalemate. White cannot win this ending unless his king is already close to the Black pawn.

PAWNS VERSUS PAWNS

When only kings and pawns remain on the board, when the pawns are equal, and when no pawn is passed, the outcome depends

III-16   **Drawn Game**

on the position of the kings. In Diagram III-16, the player to move can seize the opposition and then win the adverse pawn, but this does not suffice for a win. Therefore, White to move plays 1 K-B4 and captures the Black pawn (by the process shown in the next section), but Black need only be prepared to answer KxP by K-Q2, and the draw is assured.

III-17   **White to Move Wins**

In Diagram III-17, White to move wins by:

1 K-B4	K-K3	4 K-B6	K-Q2
2 K-N5	K-K2	5 K-K5	K-B3
3 K-B5	K-Q3	6 K-K6	

Now the Black king has to forsake his pawns, and White captures both of them. With two passed pawns, White has an easy win. Comparison of III-16 with III-17 emphasizes a general principle; superior king position is likely to count for more if there are several pawns on each side (none passed) than if there is only one.

Divided Pawns.   When the pawns are divided into two widely separated groups, a queening race many ensue.   In Diagram

III-18   The Player to Move Wins

III-18, White takes the opposition with 1 K-K4 and is sure to penetrate to one Black pawn or the other. In doing so, he lets the Black king past to attack on the opposite wing. White's victory is only a matter of time. Thus:

1 K-K4	K-Q3	5 P-N5	K-R6!
2 K-B5	K-Q4	6 P-N6	P-N5
3 KxP	K-B5	7 P-N7	P-N6
4 K-B4	KxP	8 P queens	P-N7

White wins as shown in III-13.

In III-18 Black has an alternative line of defense that brings out another principle of attack.

1 K-K4	K-K2
2 K-B5	K-B2
3 KxP	K-N2

Now Black can prevent the KNP from queening. White should not dally on the K-side but should cross over at once to the Q-side to capture the other Black pawn. The KNP is left behind as a "decoy." (This is the usual term, but a term such as "leash" or "manacle" would be more appropriate.) Before the Black king can go to the Q-side, he has to capture the KNP, wherefore he arrives on the Q-side much too late to stop the QNP.

One Pawn Plus. With only pawns left on the board, a preponderance of one pawn is generally a win, though there are some exceptions. The stronger side should (a) beware of exchanging pawns in such a manner as to be left with one pawn that he cannot queen and (b) beware of expending reserve pawn moves prematurely. He should try to penetrate with his king until he can (a) force his extra pawn through and queen it, or (b) win additional material.

III-19   **White Wins**

These principles are exemplified in Diagram III-19. A mistake would be 1 P-Q5ch. After 1 . . . K-B3, Black has the opposition, and White can make no headway. For example, 2 P-K5ch, PxPch 3 K-K4, K-K2 4 KxP, K-Q2 and draws. Or 2 K-N4, K-N3! (not 2 . . . K-K4 3 K-B3, K-B3 4 K-B4, and White has gained the opposition) 3 K-R4, K-B3! (not 3 . . . K-R3 4 P-K5, K-N3 5 P-K6 with an easy win. In this line 4 . . . PxP 5 P-Q6 wins because the Black king cannot get inside the square of queening) 4 K-N4, K-N3, drawn. The right continuation from III-19 is:

1   K-N5   K-B2

Observe once and for all that 1 . . . P-Q4 in such positions is useless. White is not so kind as to reply PxP. He moves P-K5, and the protected passed pawn wins easily.

2   K-B5   K-K2
3   K-N6   K-K3
4   P-Q5ch

This advance is good, even though it loses the KP.

4 . . .   K-K4

If K-K2, then 5 K-N7 and wins the Black pawn.

And wins.

If in III-19 it is Black's turn to move and he plays 1 . . . K-B3, then 2 P-Q5 is correct. White expends his reserve move to change the opposition. If Black then retreats, White goes forward and eventually captures the Black pawn. If 2 . . . K-N3, then 3 P-K5, PxPch 4 KxP, K-B2 5 K-Q6! K-K1 6 K-B7 and wins. White has swapped pawns at a time when the Black king was just too far away to stop the QP.

REVIEW III

1. When are the two kings in (a) direct opposition? (b) diagonal opposition?

2. Each side has one passed pawn. In what way might one player find his own pawn to be a detriment?

3. Define *queening square* and *square of queening* as used in this lesson.

4. Each king stands on K1; it is White's turn to move. Which player has the distant opposition?

5. The two kings and one White pawn are on the board. State two conditions under which the pawn might be queened by force.

6. Same forces as in Question 5. What can be said of the queening prospects if the Black king stands (a) directly in front of the pawn, (b) on the same file but three or more ranks ahead of it?

7. Is your answer to 6(b) affected if the pawn is on a rook's file?

8. Each side has one pawn. The White pawn queens, then the Black pawn moves to the 7th rank, guarded by its king, also on the 7th. Can White win?

9. What exceptions must be noted in answering Question 8?

10. White has two connected pawns; Black has one pawn on the same file as one of the White. State two processes by which White might force a win.

ANSWERS TO REVIEW III

1. (a) Direct opposition when they stand on the same rank or file with one square intervening. (b) Diagonal opposition when they stand on the same diagonal with one square intervening.

2. His pawn would be a detriment if it stood on a square over which the king had to pass to catch the enemy pawn in time.

3. The queening square is that on which a pawn would queen, the 8th rank square on its file. The square of queening is the imaginary large square of which the pawn and its queening square are two corners.

4. White.

5. The pawn can be queened if (a) the Black king is too far away to catch it, or (b) the White king can gain the opposition in front of the pawn.

6. (a) The pawn can never be queened, if Black plays correctly.
   (b) Same answer as to 5 (b) unless the pawn is a rook's pawn.

7. The White pawn can never be queened if the Black king can reach any square on that file.

8. In general, White can win, but see 9.

9. Against a RP or BP White can only draw, unless his king is near enough to co-operate quickly in either capturing the Black pawn or mating after it queens.

10. According to circumstances, White might (a) force an exchange of pawns, leaving himself with the necessary opposition to queen the single pawn, or (b) use his superior control to capture the Black pawn, leaving himself two pawns ahead.

QUIZ III

1 White to move. What result?

2 Can White win?

3 Show how White can win.

4 Show how White can win.

5 Show how White wins.

6 White wins. How?

7 White to move wins. How?

8 How can White win?

9 White to move and win. How?

10 White to move and win. How?

11 White to move and win. How?

12 White to move and win. How?

13 White wins. How?

14 White wins. How?

ANSWERS TO QUIZ III

1. White wins; 1 P-R4, and the pawn queens. Although the Black king initially seems to stand within the square of queening, this

is not true, because for its first move the pawn has the privilege of jumping to the 4th rank. Its square of queening thus extends from the 3rd rank, not the 2nd.

2. Yes. Not by 1 P-N6, which stalemates, but by 1 K-N6, K-N1 2 K-R6, K-R1. Black holds the opposition, but it does him no good because the White king has reached the 6th rank. 3 P-N6, K-N1 4 P-N7, K-B2 5 K-R7 and wins. If 2 . . . K-B1, then 3 K-R7, and the pawn marches on because the danger of stalemate is averted.

3. 1 P-N5ch, K-N3 2 K-N4, K-N2 3 K-B5, K-B2 4 P-N6ch, K-N2 5 K-N5, K-N1 6 K-B6, K-B1 7 P-N7ch, K-N1 8 P-N4! In all such endings the rear pawn must be left behind to provide a reserve move at the critical juncture. 8 . . . K-R2 9 K-B7, K-R3. Now the thoughtless 10 P-N8 (Q) would stalemate. White can relieve the stalemate by 10 P-N5ch followed by queening, but more elegant is 10 P-N8 (R!) and mates in two.

4. 1 P-N7, K-R2 2 P-N8 (Q)ch, KxQ 3 K-N6, etc.

5. It is important to note that White cannot win by sacrificing his passed pawn to win the Black pawn: 1 K-N3, K-N4 2 P-K6, K-B3 3 K-B4, KxP 4 K-N5. White gets the Black pawn, but Black moves K-Q2 as soon as the pawn is captured and holds the opposition for a draw. The right line must be to penetrate on the Q-side, taking advantage of the fact that the Black king can not stray too far from the passed pawn: 1 K-K3, K-K3 2 K-Q3, K-Q2 3 K-B3, K-B3 4 K-N4, K-N3, 5 K-R4! Black cannot oppose by K-R3, for then he steps outside the square of queening. Consequently Black must give way, whereupon White moves 6 K-R5 (or N5) and soon wins the Black pawn while keeping both of his own.

6. 1 P-R4, K-B4 2 P-R5, K-N4 3 P-R6, KxP 4 KxP, K-N3 5 K-Q4, K-B3 6 K-K4, K-Q3 7 KxP, K-K3 8 K-N5 and queens his pawn. The problem illustrates a principle of fundamental importance: when each player has a passed pawn, with other pawns on the board, the player whose pawn is outside (most remote from the other pawns) has an advantage often sufficient to win. The reason is that, if both passed pawns are captured, his own king is inside and so can attack the remaining adverse pawns before the enemy king can get back to them.

7. 1 P-N4, P-N4 2 P-N5, P-N5 3 P-N6, P-N6 4 P-N7, P-N7 5 P queens, P queens 6 Q-R7ch and captures the Black queen. When

both sides queen, the first queen often wins through more or less accidental circumstances that enable her to win the second queen or to force a mate.

8. 1 P-N6, BPxP 2 P-R6, NPxP 3 P-B6 (or 1 . . . RPxP 2 P-B6, NPxP 3 P-R6). By sacrificing two pawns, White forces one past. This process is feasible, of course, only when the White pawns are so far advanced as to win the queening race and when the Black king stands outside the square of queening. This position is a noteworthy exception to the general rule that a group of pawns faced by an equal number of enemy pawns cannot, without help, force a passed pawn.

9. Why not 1 K-B3, K-K4 2 K-N4, K-Q4 3 KxP and wins? The answer is that Black has the cute defense of 1 . . . P-R6! Now if 2 PxP, the Black king reaches QB1 in plenty of time to draw against the RP. White's only hope is to maintain his pawn on the N-file. So try 2 P-N4, K-K4 3 K-N3, K-Q4 4 KxP, K-B3 5 K-R4, K-N3 and draws. The right line is K-N1! Now, if 1 . . . K-K4, 2 K-R2, K-Q4 3 K-R3, K-B4 4 KxP and wins. Black is constrained to try the diversion 1 . . . P-R6, then 2 P-N3! (P-N4 uses up the pawn's vital reserve move) 2 . . . K-K4 3 K-R2, K-Q4 4 KxP, K-B4 5 K-R4 and wins.

10. 1 KxBP! (KxNP merely draws) KxP 2 K-N6, K-B5 3 K-R5. This produces a well-known deadlock in which the player to move loses, because he has to abandon the defense of his pawn.

11. Note that if 1 K-B3, K-K4, and the position becomes a deadlock as in Problem 10. White, having to move, loses his KP and the game. The right move is 1 K-B2! The Black king is unable to temporize in a similar way; whether he moves 1 . . . K-K4 or K-N3, White plays 2 K-B3 and wins, e.g., 1 . . . K-N3 2 K-B3, K-B2 3 KxP, K-B3 4 P-K5ch, PxPch 5 K-K4 (another kind of deadlock!) K-B2 6 KxP, K-K2 7 K-B5, K-Q3 8 K-N5, KxP 9 KxP, K-K3 10 K-N6.

12. You should find this problem easy after seeing the deadlock principle of the last two problems. 1 K-K3! K-Q4 2 P-R3! (P-R4 would actually lose!) P-R4 3 P-R4, K-K3 4 KxP and wins.

13. 1 Q-R3ch, K-N8 2 K-N3, P queens 3 Q-R2 mate.

14. 1 Q-Q3, K-N7 2 K-N4, P queens 3 Q-Q2ch, K-N8 4 K-N3 and Black cannot escape mate. This ending is no figment of the imagination; it has occurred in a number of master games.

Lesson IV

MINOR TACTICS

In the previous lessons, many points of tactics were illustrated, but only one was discussed (*opposition*, Lesson III). It is now time to survey the whole field of minor tactics and to learn the meaning of many common chess terms.

ATTACK

White and Black begin play with equal forces; the material balance can be altered only by captures. The most elementary tactical operation is the threat to capture an enemy unit. This we shall call an *attack*—a very restricted sense of the term. After the opening

IV-1   **The Knight Attacks**

moves (*King's Knight Opening*) 1 P-K4, P-K4 2 N-KB3 (Diagram IV-1) the knight threatens to capture the Black pawn. This is an attack as we have defined it.

When attacked, ask yourself two questions: (a) Must I parry this attack? (b) If so, what is the best method? Neophytes are prone to forget the first question and as a result to be intimidated by shadow threats, attacks that cannot be executed advantageously.

At the outset we shall deal only with real attacks. The second question is often scamped even by experienced players, who forget to review the entire list of possibilities.

The possible methods of meeting an attack are:

(a) To withdraw the attacked piece from its post.

(b) To guard it.

(c) To capture or paralyze the attacker.

(d) To intercept the line of an attacking queen, rook or bishop.

(e) To counterattack an enemy piece.

(f) To create a diversion.

All these tactical procedures are discussed in the following sections.

WITHDRAWAL

Withdrawal of the attacked unit is the simplest parry, though often the least desirable. However, it is often forced because the attacked piece is more valuable than the attacker. After the opening

IV-2   The Attacked Knight Must Move

moves (*Alekhine's Defense*) 1 P-K4, N-KB3 2 P-K5, Black cannot leave the knight to be taken (Diagram IV-2). It is true that he would capture the pawn in return, but the pawn is of less value than the knight. Hence the knight leaves his post (usually 2 . . . N-Q4).

Returning to IV-1, we see that the Black pawn cannot withdraw from the attack. The only parry is to guard it by 2 . . . N-QB3 (best) or 2 . . . P-Q3 (inferior, since it locks in the KB). Guarding is the natural parry to the attack by a superior piece against an inferior.

The Essential Guard. After the opening moves (*Ruy Lopez*) 1 P-K4, P-K4 2 N-KB3, N-QB3 3 B-N5 (Diagram IV-3), the Black

IV-3   **The Essential Guard**

KP is under attack but is adequately guarded. Likewise the Black QN is under attack but is adequately guarded. Yet the sequence 4 BxN, PxB 5 NxP does threaten to win a pawn (temporarily). The reason is that the Black QN is an *essential guard;* its disappearance would lead to loss on another square (which we will call the *focus*). When an essential guard is attacked, therefore, to guard the guard may be insufficient; reinforcement may be needed at the focus. The beginner is apt to make tactical errors by overlooking this circumstance. (We will revert to this position later.)

IV-4   **A Skirmish of
                         Attack and Guard**

In Diagram IV-4, Black moves 1 . . . QR-N1, attacking the
White QNP a second time. Unable to advance without loss, the
pawn has to be defended where it stands. The immediate 2 N-Q2
is no good, because a third attacker then operates (QB). White must
first play 2 BxB, PxB! then 3 N-Q2. Black continues with 3 . . .
N-K5, attacking an essential guard. Thus Black threatens NxN
followed by QxP. White cannot gain a pawn in recompense for his
QNP by 4 NxN, PxN 5 QxP, because instead Black plays 4 . . . QxP
at once. Then if 5 QxQ, RxQ, and Black attacks the QB as well as
the knight and is bound to regain his piece and remain with a pawn
plus. Or if 5 N-Q2, Black regains his piece by 5 . . . QxB (or better
5 . . . QxQ, the White queen being an essential guard of the bishop,
6 NxQ, RxB). After 3 . . . N-K5, White therefore defends by 4
KN-B3. This move illustrates the situation in which guarding the
guard is adequate at the focus: the second guard has the same powers
as the first (e.g., 4 . . . NxN 5 NxN and the QNP is still protected).
Black makes a preparatory move 4 . . . P-KB4, and White moves 5
KR-N1. Next 5 . . . Q-N4, and, if White pauses to protect his KP,
Black continues P-KN4 threatening P-N5, and this attack on the guard
of the guard finally wins the QNP. (White did not wait to be strangled
but lashed back with 5 NxN, giving up the pawn at once but failing
to save the game.)

Overload. When one piece is charged with the duty of guarding essentially two or more foci, the burden may prove an *overload*.

IV-5   **Beware of Overload**

In Diagram IV-5, if White moves 1 R-B5, the attacked knight should withdraw; to guard it by 1 . . . R-K3 would be an error, since that overloads the rook. White can continue 2 NxP, since, if 2 . . . RxN, then 3 RxN, and White remains a pawn ahead.

IV-6   **White to Play and Win**

Overloading may bring trouble in many guises. A trap from the *Three Knights Opening* is shown in Diagram IV-6. Black's QB3 seems adequately guarded by P, N, and Q. The queen, not even attacked, is guarded by the knight. Yet there is an overload, as White demonstrates by 1 NxN. Now if 1 . . . QxQ 2 NxNch, and White wins a piece. The same reply scotches 1 . . . QxB. The Black knight cannot recapture, for he must maintain guard of the queen. Hence 1 . . . PxN is forced. Then 2 QxQ, and, since the knight must maintain guard of QB3, the reply 2 . . . PxQ is forced. Now the White KB is relieved of siege, the Black knight is left in an awkward post bereft of friends, and 3 B-R3 wins the exchange.

Multiple Attack and Guard. When a piece is several times attacked and several times guarded, how do you determine whether it is safe from loss? One way, of course, is to play out mentally the sequence of captures and recaptures to see what the upshot will be. A simpler way is often possible: count and compare the number of attackers and guards. If there are more attackers, the attacking side can capture first and last and thus gain a unit. If the guards equal

IV-7 Multiple Attack and Guard

the attackers, they will make the last capture and so restore equality. Consider Diagram IV-7. The QP is assailed by two knights, a bishop, and three heavy pieces — total 6. Black therefore threatens to win the pawn; White must defend again by N-K2.

The foregoing rule suffices only if it is clear that neither side will be compelled (in its effort to restore equality) to expose a superior piece to capture by an inferior. Gain of a *unit* is not worth the cost of loss of *force*. Picture Diagram IV-7 with the Black queen and the rook at Q3 interchanged. Then if 1 . . . NxP, 2 NxN, NxN 3 BxN, BxB 4 RxB, QxR 5 RxQ, RxR, White is not so obliging as to continue 6 QxR, RxQ; he breaks off the series of captures (as by 6 Q-N3), and Black is left with R+R+P versus Q+N. White should win.

INTERPOSITION

A way of parrying an attack from a queen, rook, or bishop is to *interpose* a piece on the line of attack. Naturally this tactic is feasible only if (a) the interposed piece is adequately guarded and (b) it is not more valuable than the attacker.

IV-8   **The Prussian Attack**

After the opening moves (*Prussian Attack* in the *Two Knights Defense*) 1 P-K4, P-K4 2 N-KB3, N-QB3 3 B-B4, N-B3 4 N-N5 (Diagram IV-8) the Black KBP is twice attacked. The usual parry is the interposition 4 . . . P-Q4, so that if 5 BxP, NxB, and the attack is over. (White can continue 5 PxP, N-QR4 6 B-N5ch, P-B3 7 PxP, PxP 8 B-K2; the soundness of the *Two Knights Defense* depends on whether Black now gains a lead in development sufficient to compensate for his loss of a pawn.)

OBSTRUCTION

Interposition may be used for offensive purposes, but in that case we usually call it *obstruction*. In Diagram IV-9 the Black king is in

IV-9   **White to Win**

a precarious position. Were the White bishop at K2, then 1 B-B4ch, K-R1 2 QxBch would lead to mate. This fact suggests trying 1 B-B7ch, K-R1 2 B-B4, but then Black has time to defend the bishop again (2 . . . Q-K2 or B1) or move the bishop away (2 . . . B-K2). After 1 B-B7ch, K-R1, White therefore makes the obstructing move 2 B-K8! Now 2 . . . B-K2 is useless because 3 Q-B8ch still mates; likewise 2 . . . BxPch 3 QxB, RxB 4 Q-B8ch mates; or 2 . . . RxB 3 QxBch. Black can but give up his bishop (2 . . . P-KR4) to live a little longer.

IV-10   **White to Win**

Obstruction can appear in forms other than interposition. The posting of a piece in front of an enemy pawn is a form of obstruction in that the piece prevents the pawn's advance. Also, there is such a thing as inducing *self-obstruction*. In Diagram IV-10 White might try 1 B-Q3, threatening a tremendous double check. But Black makes the anticipatory interposition 1 . . . P-KB4 and can then weather the storm. Therefore 1 N-B6ch! forcing 1 . . . BxN. Now the bishop obstructs his own pawn, so that 2 B-Q3ch forces R-N3 (not 2 . . . K-R1 3 QxP mate). With 3 P-R5 White wins at least the rook in return for the knight sacrificed.

FORK

A *fork* is a simultaneous attack by one piece on two or more enemy pieces. For example, after the opening moves (*Two Knights Defense*) 1 P-K4, P-K4 2 N-KB3, N-QB3 3 B-B4, N-B3 4 N-B3

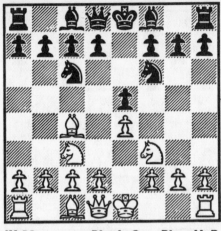

IV-11   **Black Can Play NxP**

(Diagram IV-11), Black's best move is 4 . . . NxP. After 5 NxN
he regains his piece by 5 . . . P-Q4, forking the knight and bishop.

IV-12   **White to Move**

Each of the pieces is capable of double attack, even the king.
For example, in Diagram IV-12, winning a pawn by 1 NxPch would
be a mistake. Black moves 1 . . . K-N2 and must win one of the
pieces. Perhaps the most frequent forks — either as actual occur-
rences or as dangers to be avoided — are by the knight, in which
one of his attacks is upon the king (a check). White wins in Diagram

IV-13   **The Royal Fork**

IV-13 by 1 QxR! for if 1 . . . QxQ, 2 N-K7ch, K-Q1 (or N1) 3
N(either)xQBPch, PxN 4 NxPch, K moves 5 NxQ, White recovers
the queen and remains material ahead.

CHECK

Many checks are of course a prelude to mate or to gaining material.   After the opening moves 1 P-K4, P-K4 2 N-KB3, defending

IV-14   **White to Win**

the KP by 2 . . . P-KB3 is unsound (Diagram IV-14), for White can
play 3 NxP anyway. If 3 . . . PxN, then 4 Q-R5ch, and this check

is singularly difficult to meet. The natural move 4 . . . P-KN3 allows 5 QxKPch, forking king and rook. But if 4 . . . K-K2 5 QxKPch, K-B2 6 B-B4ch, and the king cannot long survive.

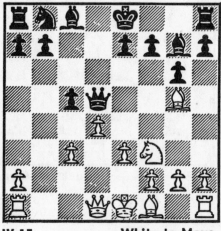

IV-15   **White to Move**

Many checks, on the other hand, have more modest aims — to develop with gain of time, to post a piece on a strong square, to force an awkward move by the opponent. In Diagram IV-15 (a regular position of the *Gruenfeld Defense*) the "book" move is 1 B-N5ch. There is no thought here of assaulting the Black king; the idea is to clear the way for castling without loss of time. If 1 B-K2 (or Q3), Black might continue 1 . . . PxP 2 BPxP, Q-R4ch 3 Q-Q2, QxQch 4 NxQ, P-K4 with great advantage. The check gives White time to steer into other channels: e. g., 1 . . . B-Q2 2 P-B4, Q-K5 3 O-O.

Discovered Check. A discovered check is one given by a queen, rook, or bishop by removal of a friendly piece from the line between it and the enemy king. Many discovered checks are extremely dangerous, for the masking piece can hurl itself into your territory, though attacked a dozen times: you have no time to capture it because you must first cover the check. After the opening moves (*Petroff Defense*) 1 P-K4, P-K4 2 N-KB3, N-KB3 3 NxP, NxP? (playable,

IV-16   **Black to Move**

but inferior to P-Q3) 4 Q-K2 (Diagram IV-16), withdrawal of the
attacked knight (4 . . . N-KB3) is catastrophic; White plays 5 N-B6ch
(discovered) and wins the queen. (The right defense is 4 . . . Q-K2
5 QxN, P-Q3 recovering the piece, though losing a pawn.)

Double Check. A double check is a particularly vicious discovered check in which the masking piece also gives check. The only
possible reply is to move the king; if the king is immobile, he is mated,
even though both attacking pieces are themselves attacked. In Dia-

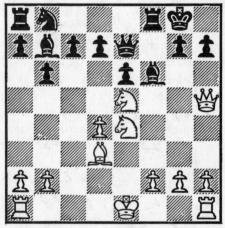

IV-17 White Announced Mate in 8

gram IV-17 observe that NxBch, opening an attack from the White KB on the KRP, leads to nothing; 1 . . . PxN opens the rank for the queen to guard KR2. Nor does 1 N-N5 avail, for 1 . . . P-N3 saves the day. White played 1 QxPch! KxQ 2 NxBch (double). The force of this sequence is twofold: (a) it drives the Black king into the open (2 . . . K-R1? 3 N-N6 mate) and (b) it destroys the strong defensive bishop without allowing recapture. Forced mate follows: 2 . . . K-R3 3 N(5)-N4ch, K-N4 4 P-R4ch, K-B5 5 P-N3ch, K-B6 6 B-K2ch, K-N7 7 R-R2ch, K-N8 8 K-Q2 mate.

PIN

A *pin* is the total or partial immobilization of a piece through the circumstance that its move off the line would expose a friendly

IV-18   **Absolute Pin**

piece to the attack of an enemy queen, rook, or bishop. In Diagram IV-18 the Black QN is *absolutely* pinned; to move it, exposing the king to capture, would be illegal. In Diagram IV-19 the Black KN

IV-19   **Relative Pin**

is *relatively* pinned; that is, he may legally move, but such a move would result in the loss of the queen for the less valuable bishop.

IV-20   **Line Pins**

The knight is *wholly* pinned, if at all. Each of the other pieces, however, may be *line-pinned,* that is, be held to a fixed line but still be capable of moving upon it. Diagram IV-20 shows line-pinned Black pieces in three corners; the rook, queen, and bishop are able to move on the line and capture the pinning piece. Even the lowly pawn may be line-pinned, vertically or diagonally. At the upper right, the pawn could capture the queen but for the bishop or could capture the pinning bishop if it were not for the check. Evidently, the queen alone can never be wholly pinned, only line-pinned.

The Legal Mate. Never overlook the difference between an absolute and a relative pin! Undue reliance on a relative pin leads to many catastrophes, of which the following is a prototype: 1 P-K4, P-K4 2 N-KB3, P-Q3 3 B-B4, B-N5? (premature) 4 N-B3, P-KN3??

IV-21 **The Legal Mate**

(Diagram IV-21). Now White wins. 5 NxP! If 5 . . . PxN 6 QxB leaves White a healthy pawn ahead. But if 5 . . . BxQ then 6 BxPch, K-K2 7 N-Q5 mate. (This *Legal Mate* is so called because first demonstrated by a French player, the Sire de Legal, about 1750.)

Unpin. A pin usually hampers the victim and is sometimes a serious menace. To dissolve it quickly is often desirable or imperative. The methods of unpin are: (a) to interpose on the line a piece of value no greater than the pinner, (b) to move the rearward piece off the line, and (c) to drive away the pinner.

Reverting to Diagram IV-18, we note that this is a regular position of the *Ruy Lopez* (*Steinitz Defense*). Black has just moved 2 . . . P-Q3, a "self-pin." The idea is to follow immediately with B-Q2, unpinning by interposition while still keeping the KP guarded. In certain circumstances, Black might dispense with 3 . . . B-Q2 and instead move out his K-side pieces to play O-O; this is an instance of the (b) process. In IV-19 Black might move Q-Q2 (after developing his QB) as a (b) operation, but this is open to the objection that White's BxN then doubles his KBP. The appropriate course is (c), by 1 . . . P-KR3. The exchange 2 BxN, QxB is good for Black; the retreat 2 B-K3 convicts White's last move (B-N5) of being a loss of time, while 2 B-R4, P-KN4 lifts the siege. After Black has played O-O, this operation (. . . P-KR3 and . . . P-KN4) is usually bad, for it seriously exposes the king; but in IV-19 it is feasible because Black can castle on the Q-side, then continue his K-side pawn storm.

COUNTERATTACK

Attack is used in the lesson in a restricted sense — a threat to capture a piece. *Counterattack* is similarly used in a restricted sense — the reply to an attack by an attack on a piece of equal value. After the opening move 1 P-K4, P-K4 2 N-KB3, N-QB3 3 B-B4, N-B3

IV-22   **Counterattack**

4 P-Q4, PxP 5 P-K5 (Diagram IV-22) Black may withdraw his knight, attacked as it is by a pawn. Better than the immediate withdrawal, however, is the counterattack 5 . . . P-Q4, so that if 6 PxN then PxB. Black has opened the door for his QB and also has guarded his K5 in case of 6 B-N5 or N3, N-K5. (Least desirable for White is 6 PxPe.p., BxP.)

IV-23   Faulty Counterattack

A maxim to paste in your hat is: before embarking on a counterattack, canvass the whole board, for being the *second player* in a
potential series of captures and compensating captures involves the
risk that the *first player* will be able to interrupt the series in such a
way as to prevent you from equalizing. The most drastic interruption
is of course a check. In Diagram IV-23, White has just moved
R(QR1)-B1, seizing an open file without loss of time because of the
attack on the Black queen. To attempt to seize an open file in return,
by 1 . . . KR-K1, would be a fatal blunder. White does not oblige
by 2 RxQ, RxQ with equality, but skips lightly away by 2 Q-N3ch,
followed by 3 RxQ, winning material.

IV-24   **The Desperado**

The Desperado. In Diagram IV-24, Black has just answered the attack on his rook by the counterattack B-Q4, so that if 1 NxR, BxR. But White can instead play 1 RxP. Under normal circumstances, to give up a rook for a pawn would be a great loss, but here, after 1 . . . PxR 2 NxR, White regains his piece and has won a pawn. A piece that can thus afford to give up its life for whatever it can get, because of the attack on a like piece, has been picturesquely dubbed *desperado.*

A constant hazard of counterattack for the *second player* is that the *first player's* attacked piece becomes desperado. Black's move B-Q4 (from B3) was faulty.

The Raid. A *raid* is a series of captures, countered by a series of equalizing captures. It is usually precipitated by a counterattack and likewise involves a continual hazard for the *second player.** The choice rests with the *first player* whether to continue a raid or to end it by capturing the enemy raider.

---

*Since the roles may be exchanged, keep in mind this distinction: the *first player* is he whose capture *gains* material; the *second* is he whose capture merely *restores equality.*

IV-25   **White to Move**

In Diagram IV-25, Black threatens NxP, forking queen and rook. White rejects 1 BxN because his two knights would be inferior to the Black bishops. What about 1 RxB, RxR 2 P-K4 with the idea of gaining two minor pieces for a rook? This is seen to be no good; Black's rook would be desperado, so that 2 . . . RxN 3 PxR, N-K6 with a winning game. The right move is 1 N-B6. Black cannot reply by withdrawing the queen, for the queen is overloaded: 1 . . . Q-Q2? 2 BxN, QxB 3 NxB. Therefore Black has to accede to a raid with 1 . . . NxP 2 NxQ, NxQ. The raid is halted for the moment, since both raiders have run out of prey. White might end it once and for all with 3 QRxN, QRxN, but then Black remains a pawn up. Happily, White can withdraw his raider with a new attack: 3 N-B6. Black has no adequate counterattack: e.g., 3 . . . N-K6 4 NxB, NxR 5 RxN, and White has two minor pieces against a rook. (Black tried a diversion but could not escape this outcome: 3 . . . B-N4 4 KRxN! B-K6ch 5 K-R1, B-N5 6 N-B1, BxR 7 RxB.)

IV-26   **White to Move**

A striking example of the plight of the second player in a raid is Diagram IV-26. Black is hard put to save his pinned KB. He tries a counterattack on the White queen (R-N2), but it proves insufficient: 1 RxB, RxQ (forced) 2 RxQ, RxB (again forced; any time the Black rook quits and saves itself, so does the White rook, and White remains a piece ahead) 3 R-Q6, RxB (forced) 4 RPxR. At last White ends the raid; he emerges from the exchange ahead by enough to win the game.

COMPENSATING ATTACK

When threatened with the loss of a unit, you can sometimes let the unit go if you can then execute a *compensating attack* that will win a like unit. Let us look again at Diagram IV-3, reproduced on the following page.

We pointed out that the Black knight is an essential guard; the attack on it by the White bishop threatens to win the KP. One way of parrying the attack is by bringing another guard to the focus by 3 . . . P-Q3 (Diagram IV-18). But if you have duly asked yourself the first question: Must I parry this attack? you should discover that the answer is no. Suppose that White is free to execute his threat: 4 BxN, QPxB 5 NxP, then 5 . . . Q-Q5 forks knight and pawn and must win the latter. This compensating attack is inherent in the position, and Black need not worry about his KP until White has brought more force to bear on the center (as by P-Q3 or N-QB3). The usual move, indeed, is 3 . . . P-QR3, "putting the question" to the bishop. If 4 B-R4 to maintain the attack, Black is able to lift it at will by P-QN4.

IV-27   **White to Move**

If you conscientiously ask yourself the first question, you will be surprised to discover how many adverse threats can be ignored because a compensating attack lies at hand. Diagram IV-27 is a regular position of the *Evans Gambit*. White has sacrificed a pawn for rapid development. Black has just moved N-R4. Must White pause to defend his KB? No, for, if NxB, then White regains the piece by the fork Q-R4ch. White can therefore go ahead with his K-side assault. (Both N-KN5 and B-KN5 have been played.)

A compensating attack is clearly akin to a counterattack. The distinction is that the offsetting captures are consecutive in counterattack; in a compensating attack, at least one non-capturing move intervenes.

THE DIVERSION

The last item on our list of possible ways of meeting an attack is "to create a diversion." By this we mean to make a counterthreat at least as serious as the opponent's. In Diagram IV-28, a regular

IV-28   **The Diversion**

position of *King's Gambit Declined,* Black has just moved N-Q5, attacking the queen and also threatening a fork of king and rook by NxPch. White can, of course, hold everything by 1 Q-Q1—an unenterprising retreat. The book move is 1 Q-N3, establishing a threat at least as serious as Black's: e.g., 1 . . . NxPch 2 K-Q1, NxR 3 QxP, R-B1 4 PxP, PxP 5 B-N5, B-K2 6 R-B1. The verdict of experience is that White emerges from the bloodletting with the better game. If Black wants to avoid this variation, he must pause for a defensive move, as 1 . . . Q-K2, whereupon White can parry the threat by 2 K-Q1 (or 2 PxP, PxP 3 K-Q1). The forfeiture of castling is a small price to pay for maintaining the aggressive position of the queen.

In this example, White's diversion does not prevent Black from executing his threat but prepares a counterattack that will restore White to material or positional equality if not superiority. In other instances, a diversion is a positive parry, as when a threat to win a piece is met by a counterthreat to checkmate. Thus the necessity for finding another parry is delayed for one or more moves and sometimes evaporates.

Every *Zwischenzug* (a move interpolated before a necessary or expected move, exerting a threat that the opponent cannot ignore) is by definition diversionary. In the variation of IV-28 1 Q-N3, Q-K2 2 K-Q1, White's first move stands as a *Zwischenzug* inserted before the necessary K-Q1. (The book recommends insertion of a second *Zwischenzug* 2 PxP, clearing the diagonal for White to move B-KN5 with threat of N-Q5. If 2 . . . NxPch 3 K-Q1, NxR, then 4 PxN, and White will win two knights for his rook.)

REVIEW IV

1. What is a simultaneous attack on two separate points usually called?
2. What parry by a bishop is not possible to an attack by a knight?
3. How does a relative pin differ from an absolute pin as we have used the terms?
4. Name at least four of the six tactical devices we have enumerated as possible answers to an attack.
5. What is a *Zwischenzug?*
6. What piece can never be completely immobilized by a pin?
7. Define counterattack as used in this lesson.
8. What is the difference between a counterattack and a compensating attack?
9. Of the ways of answering an attack upon a piece, which are not possible when that piece is the king?
10. A desperado is a piece that can afford to sacrifice itself to capture an inferior piece. How does it get that way?

ANSWERS TO REVIEW IV

1. Fork.
2. Interposition.
3. A pin is absolute when the rearward piece is the king; to move off the line, exposing the king to check, is illegal. A pin is relative when a move off the line would allow a superior piece to be captured at the cost of an inferior.
4. The six ways (in brief) are: withdrawal, guard, capture or pin of the attacker, interposition, counterattack, and diversion.
5. A move interpolated before a practically necessary move, as before a return capture that is necessary to restore equality of force.
6. The queen, which can only be line-pinned.
7. A counterattack is a threat to capture an enemy piece of value equal to one's own attacked piece.
8. A counterattack, if carried through, would answer a capture; in a compensating attack, at least one noncapturing move intervenes

between the capture by one side and the countercapture by the other.

9. Guard, pin of the attacker, counterattack, and diversion.

10. Because an enemy piece of value equal to the desperado is under attack.

QUIZ IV

1 White can win material. How?

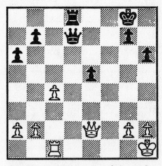

2 Can White safely take the KP?

3 White can win a pawn. How?

4 In the regular position of the *Ruy Lopez* opening, White may play PxP. Why does not this move lose material?

5 Black to move. Why is K-N2 not good?

6 How can Black win quickly?

7 White can draw. How?

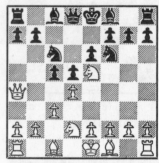

8 Black moved 1 . . . B-K2. Why could he afford to ignore White's threat to win a pawn by 2 NxN, PxN 3 QxPch?

9 Show how Black can win a pawn.

10 White to move. (See question below.)

10 (a) The Black queen is an essential guard to the bishop and
        the knight but is not overloaded. Why?
    (b) White can attack the essential guard by 1 Q-B7. How
        can Black answer this move?
    (c) How could Black answer 1 Q-B4?
    (b) How could Black answer 1 N-K5?

ANSWERS TO QUIZ IV

1. 1 R-R8ch, KxR 2 NxPch and 3 NxQ.
2. Yes, because, after 1 QxP, Q-Q8ch, White does not answer 2
    RxQ, which would lead to mate, but 2 Q-K1.
3. Q-B2 forks the QBP and KRP; Black cannot save both.
4. Because, if 1 . . . NxB, White wins back a piece by the com-
    pensating attack 2 P-QR4. The knight has no safe square of
    withdrawal.
5. K-N2 is not good, because it leaves the king overloaded, having
    to guard the knight and KRP: 2 BxNch, KxB 3 NxPch wins
    a pawn.
6. 1 . . . RxPch 2 RxR, QxQ. Because of the pin, White cannot
    reply RxQ and therefore loses his queen for a rook.
7. This is an important ending that demonstrates the drawing power
    of the knight against an advanced pawn.   1 N-R4, so that, if the
    pawn queens, 2 N-B3ch captures it.   Since the knight threatens
    to settle on N2 to guard the queening square, Black can only try
    to chase the knight away: 1 . . . K-K6 2 N-N2ch, K-B7 (use-
    less is 2 . . . K-B6 3 N-K1ch, K-B7 4 N-B2) 3 N-B4.   Again,
    if the pawn queens, it is captured by a fork, 4 N-Q3ch, but, if
    the pawn does not move, then 4 NxP, draw.
8. If 2 NxN, Black has the reply Q-Q2, pinning the knight and
    also bringing another piece to the guard of his QB3. On the
    next move he can play QxN or PxN and has lost nothing.
9. 1 . . . NxBP! Then if 2 QxN, QxQ 3 RxQ, BxN. Or if 2
    RxN, QxN. In either case the White bishop is pinned under
    the penalty of RxR mate, so that the White knight is loose.
10. (a) The Black queen is not overloaded, because, if White cap-
    tures either the bishop or the knight, recapture by the queen
    leaves her still guarding the other piece. This is one of several

situations to remember in which an essential guard can do double duty.

(b) One way would be to retreat the knight, for then 2 QxQ, BxQ, and the bishop also withdraws from attack. Observe that this double withdrawal is possible because the Black queen and bishop guard each other. For the same reason, Black could make such a move as 1 . . . K-R2, for 2 QxQ is not actually a threat to win a piece, being answered by 2 . . . BxQ, guarding the knight. But then White would gain time by an attack on the bishop, 3 R-B7 (threatening RxB followed by BxN) to win at least the QRP.

(c) 1 . . . B-Q3 withdraws the attacked bishop and pins the White bishop that attacks the knight. If 2 BxB, White cannot follow by 3 QxN because 2 . . . QxB is a check. Thus Black gains a tempo to save his knight. Of course, 2 QxN? loses to QxQ.

(d) White's threat is, of course, 2 BxN and 3 N-N6ch with a mighty fork. This is no threat as long as Black can answer BxN with QxNch but will become serious if White is given time to guard his knight, as by Q-K4. Black must immediately prepare to destroy or oust the knight: 1 . . . B-Q3.

Lesson V

MATING COMBINATIONS: PART ONE

In Lesson IV you were introduced to the minor tactics of chess. The present lesson will illustrate through many examples how the tactics are co-ordinated in *mating combinations*. A *mating combination* is a line of play that results in either (a) checkmate, or (b) a decisive gain of material through the threat of mate.

DEALING THE DEATH BLOW

We will begin with positions in which one player is already beaten strategically—the only question is how to effect mate quickly. Here we are concerned with only the simplest applications of tactics.

Obstruction. In Diagram V-1, Black has made material sacrifice to get his KBP to the 7th rank and to bottle up the White king.

V-1   **Black to Move**

Now he must find a quick win, or else he himself will be mated by Q-B6ch, etc. All that prevents his KBP from going to the 8th rank is the queen's command of the file. The solution then is the obstruction 1 . . . B-B5ch. If 2 NxB, the queen is obstructed, so that 2 . . . P-B8(N) is mate. (Do not forget that a promoting pawn can be replaced by any piece you choose!) If 2 QxB, PxQ, Black has decisive superiority of force.

Pin. In Diagram V-2, only the Black queen prevents White from mating by Q-K7. Can the Black queen be neutralized? Well,

V-2   **White to Move**

let us try the obvious move 1 R-B8. We observe that 1 . . . BxR is no good, for the interference with the QR allows QxQ mate. Therefore Black must play 1 . . . RxR. But after 2 RxR Black cannot parry both threats, 3 Q-K7 and 3 QxQ.

Decoy of Guard. In Diagram V-3, Black would like to continue his attack by 1 . . . BxPch, but the White queen guards the pawn

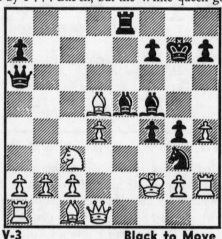

V-3   **Black to Move**

and will recapture with check. Can the queen be decoyed away? A drastic method would be 1 . . . Q-B8ch, sacrificing the queen. Let us see whether the investment will pay off: 2 QxQ, BxPch 3 B-K3. Of course, Black can capture this bishop, but BxB is not mate, the file of the Black rook being closed. How about 3 . . . RxB? This threatens 4 . . . R-K7, a double check, wherefore nothing would avail White but to find a flight square for his king—which he cannot. Therefore the sacrifice is sound.

Line-Opening. In Diagram V-4, Black has just made the mistake of castling. White plays 1 QxPch, PxQ 2 B-R6 mate. It is

V-4   **White to Move**

worth a queen to displace the QNP, opening the diagonal for a check, since this check happens to be mate. (If you think this a mere happenstance, be advised that this combination after O-O-O has been executed a number of times in master play; it is a constant hazard in certain regular opening variations.) Later we will give many more examples of sacrificial line-openings.

V-5   **White to Move**

Decoying the King. In Diagram V-5 the Black king seems fairly well sheltered, being pressed at the moment by only the White queen and KB. We might try bringing additional pieces into action, as by 1 B-K5; however, 1 . . . B-K2 seems to be an adequate answer. The move 1 R-Q8 looks strong, but with 1 . . . QxN Black wins a piece and breaks the attack. Let us therefore consider whether we can draw the Black king toward the center, where all the White pieces operate. Eureka! 1 QxNch, KxQ 2 B-K5 is mate. There remains only the question whether 1 . . . KxQ is forced. Well, if 1 . . . K-N1, obviously we can now play 2 R-Q8 (or even stronger, 2 B-K5). We win everything in sight, even if we do not mate.

V-6   **Black to Move**

The habit of examining what may look like useless sacrifices
often pays off. In Diagram V-6 Black wants to force the White
king out of his shelter. Is 1 QxPch any good? Certainly! For
then 1 . . . KxQ 2 B-R6 is mate, and, of course, if 1 . . . K-K1, White
can help himself to a rook—if he finds nothing better.

V-7   **White to Move**

After these examples, you should have no difficulty with Diagram
V-7. Clearly, strong is 1 QxPch, because 1 . . . KxQ 2 B-R5 mates
next. Hence 1 . . . K-B1, after which White must surely take a heavy
toll: e.g., 2 R-R8ch, K-K2 3 RxNch, RxR 4 QxRch, etc.

V-8   **White to Move**

More subtle is Diagram V-8. The White queen and bishops menace the Black king, but where is the mate? No other piece can be brought up quickly; but how can the positions of the queen and bishops be improved? We see that 1 Q-N4ch is useless, for then 1 . . . K-K1; the queen cannot give check and at the same time guard Black's K1. Perhaps you will see the winning idea—to draw the king away from K1, by 1 B-K6ch, KxB 2 Q-K8ch. The check does not hurt—Black has a queen and two knights to interpose—but the White queen now guards the two vital squares: Black's Q2 and KB2. The Black king is thereby immobilized, so that 3 P-Q5 is checkmate.

V-9   **Black to Move**

One of the best examples of this tactic of drawing the king away from guarding a key square is Diagram V-9. Black announced mate in four. Try to solve this problem before reading further. The solution is: 1 . . . N-K7ch (to open the file for the Black rook and at the same time decoy the White rook to K2) 2 RxN, R-B8ch! (to draw the king away from guarding his R1) 3 KxR, Q-R8ch 4 K-B2, N-N5 mate.

Self-Block. The problemists' term *self-block* means the obstruction of a king by a friendly piece standing adjacent to it. In the final position of Diagram V-9 the White king's escape to K2 is blocked by the White rook's standing there. The preliminary Black maneuvers had to decoy the rook to this square for the sake of the self-block.

V-10   **White to Move**

A similar rook-decoy is the key to *Philidor's Legacy,* a well-known combination typified by Diagram V-10. The Black king is stalemated, and 1 N-Q7 is a check, but it is not a mate, because the knight cuts off the queen's guard of Black's QB1. White mates by inducing a self-block on that square: 1 N-Q7ch, K-B1 2 N-N6ch (double), K-N1 (not K-Q1, 3 Q-Q7 mate) 3 Q-B8ch, RxQ 4 N-Q7 mate. Any such position, in which mate is delivered by a knight and the king is entirely or mostly hemmed in by his own pieces, is commonly called a *smothered mate.*

V-11   **White to Move**

Square Vacation. We come now to *clearance* maneuvers concerned with getting one's own pieces out of the way for the benefit of other pieces. A simple example is Diagram V-11. White has sacrificed a piece to rip up the Black K-side and could now even the score by PxNch. Can he do better? Well, if his queen were off the square he could move N-N7 mate (smothered). Hence, to vacate the key square without giving Black a breathing spell, White plays 1 Q-N6ch, then mates whether Black answers PxQ or R-B2.

V-12   **Black to Move**

In Diagram V-12, Black to move studies the effect of 1 . . . N-N6ch. After 2 K-N1, how can he continue? The other knight might mate at R6 *if* the queen could vacate that square yet maintain guard over White's KN2. The *if* is impossible; what is needed is to replace the queen's guard by a self-block—and this *is* possible: 2 . . . Q-N7ch 3 RxQ, N-R6 mate. The rook has unblocked White's KB2, but the mating knight guards that square.

Line Vacation. In Diagram V-13, the position of the White heavy pieces suggests a mating combination by QxPch, KxQ 2 R-R3.

V-13   **White to Move**

However, this will not be mate until the White knight is moved away to let the KR rake the whole KN-file. Since the object of a knight move would be merely to clear the line, the knight is free to land on the square where he will do the most good. Since Black threatens to spoil the party by BxR, the knight moves to K6, obstructing the bishop, whereupon the mating combination cannot be parried. (Black can only delay matters a little by 1 . . . R-B2 2 QxR.)

V-14　　　　　　　　**White to Move**

In Diagram V-14, if the White rook at KB7 were out of the way, White could deliver the terrible discovered check P-K7 and win the queen. Where shall the rook move? If 1 RxQNP, for example, 1 . . . P-Q4 intercepts the White *battery*. If 1 R-Q7, the queen skips lightly away (1 . . . Q-N3ch and 2 . . . P-Q4). How about 1 R-B8ch? Of course, 1 . . . RxR lets the battery fire, but what about 1 . . . KxR? Try 2 R-B1ch (all that is left!); then 2 . . . K-K2 fails against 3 R-B7 mate, while 2 . . . K-N1 again lets the battery fire (3 P-K7ch). Black might move 1 . . . K-R2; then 2 RxR, QxR 3 NxP should lead to an easy win; the lone queen cannot stop the KP supported by three pieces. This analysis demonstrates that 1 R-B8ch was sound.

Combined Tactics. A combination of any length is bound to involve a variety of tactical elements. In Diagram V-15 White's

V-15   **White to Move**

attack seems to be bogged down by the threats to capture his queen and his rook. Drastic measures are necessary. If 1 RxPch, KxR, the king is decoyed onto the line of the White battery; then might follow 2 NxBch, QxB! (the queen being desperado) 3 QxB! (likewise desperado) QRxQ 4 NxQ, and White emerges a piece up. Has he nothing better? Analogy with such positions as V-6 suggests examination of 1 QxPch, KxQ 2 B-R6ch, K-N1. The king is bottled up; a check will kill him. How is an effective check to be delivered? Not by 3 N-K7 since the Black knight guards that square. But Black's KB3 is unguarded; can the rook vacate it and also parry any defensive move? The only defense would be 3 . . . P-B4 (or B3), opening a flight square. But then the line of the White battery is also opened, allowing 4 N-K7 double check and mate. Therefore the whole line is sound, White's third move being a square vacation by the rook. (To forestall 3 . . . QxN, stopping the mate at ruinous cost, White actually played 3 R-N6ch. If BPxR, the double check mates, and, if RPxR, the mating knight at KB6 guards the flight square.)

V-16 **White to Move**

In Diagram V-16, the Black K-side pawn formation admits of a mate by queen and bishop alone, provided that there is no interference. The first step in clearing the way is 1 N-K7ch, QxN. The queen is decoyed away from guarding the key square, White's KR5. Now White's own rook is the only remaining obstacle. White grandly disposes of it by a sacrifice, 2 R-R8ch! KxR; then the well-known combination follows, 3 Q-R5ch, K-N1 4 B-R7ch, K-R1 5 B-N6ch, K-N1 6 Q-R7 mate, or, even quicker, 4 Q-R7ch, K-B2 5 B-N6 mate. Without loss of time, the bishop has been brought to N6 to guard Black's KB2, releasing the queen from that duty.

V-17 **White to Move**

In Diagram V-17, the Black king is clearly in jeopardy, yet Black will gain a big tempo for defense if White's attacked knight retreats: e.g., 1 N(5)-N3, B-N2, guarding the knight and clearing the way for O-O. Or 1 N(4)-B3 (counterattack), P-B3 and is safe for the moment. White works out an elegant maneuver to save his knight, clear the K-file, and prevent consolidation of the Black forces. 1 Q-N5ch! depending first of all on the overload of the Black queen. 1 . . . QxQ would allow 2 N-B6 mate. Since the Black knight also is attacked, the only defense is 1 . . . N-Q2. Then 2 KR-K1, and White threatens the murderous double check N-B6. Black must give his king a flight, so 2 . . . B-N5. Next 3 N-B6ch, K-B1 4 NxNch, RxN 5 Q-K5! finishing with a knockout fork. Black resigns, since he cannot meet the two mate threats simultaneously, QxR and Q-K8.

Double Check. Not rarely is the knockout punch a double check. The tragicomedy of Diagram V-18 has been enacted many

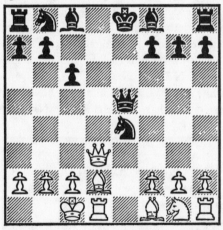

V-18 **White to Move**

times, perhaps because the position can arise in a quite natural way from the *Center Opening*. White sacrifices his queen to draw the enemy king onto the battery line: 1 Q-Q8ch, KxQ 2 B-N5ch, K-K1 3 R-Q8 mate or 2 . . . K-B2 3 B-Q8 mate.

V-19   **White to Move**

The force of the double check is, of course, that it admits of only one reply, a move of the king. Interposition, capture of a checking piece, etc. are all debarred. In Diagram V-19, White's threat of discovered check seems to be nullified by the Black knight's attack on his queen: e.g., 1 N-B6ch, NxQ 2 NxQ, N-Q5. Black's raider escapes, but White's does not. White can, however, use his battery to pave the way for a lethal double check: 1 NxQPch! NxQ 2 N-B6 mate.

V-20   **Black to Move**

In Diagram V-20, Black could mate by Q-N7, were not his own rook in the way of the bishop. If he makes a clearance move, say 1 . . . RxKB, then 2 P-B4, opening the rank for guarding KN2 with the White queen. Or if 1 . . . RxPch, not 2 RPxR, allowing the mate, but BPxR. However, there is a method that admits of no defense: 1 . . . Q-N7ch! KxQ 2 RxNP mate by double check.

PATTERNS OF COMBINATIONS

A combination to produce checkmate or material gain is necessarily based on some weakness in the enemy position. As has been said, "a combination is the discharge of accumulated advantages." All the combinations that may arise from a given type of weakness bear a family resemblance to one another. We will now turn to a study of some of the most frequent patterns.

First-Rank Mates. The pawns in front of the castled king usually defend most strongly if left unmoved. However, if the rooks get into action, if files are opened, and if minor pieces are traded off, the confinement of the king to the first rank by his own pawns may be dangerous. A rook check on the first rank will be mate if that rank is insufficiently protected.

V-21   **White to Move**

For example, in Diagram V-21 White can play 1 RxR, QxR 2 Q-R4! He forks the queen and rook and must win the latter, since 2 . . . QxQ allows 3 R-N8ch and mate next move. (White—world champion Capablanca—actually moved 1 Q-R8, and his opponent resigned, overlooking that 1 . . . RxQRP would have been an adequate defense!)

V-22   **White to Move**

All these first-rank catastrophes arise from an overload. A rook or queen that must remain on the first rank to prevent a lethal rook check cannot at the same time do guard duty on its file. In Diagram V-22, White wins by 1 N-K7ch. Since this forks the queen, the knight must be captured. The first point is that 1 . . . R(1)xN loses to 2 R-Q8ch, R-K1 3 Q-B8ch, RxQ 4 RxR mate. Therefore Black must play 1 . . . R(7)xN. The second point is that after 2 QxR Black still cannot play 2 . . . RxQ because of 3 R-Q8ch, so that White gets away with winning at least the exchange. (Actually, White can force mate unless Black gives up both his rook and his queen. The main variation is 2 . . . P-B4 3 R-Q8, RxR 4 QxRch, K-B2 5 Q-K7ch, K-N1 6 Q-B8 mate.)

V-23   **White to Move**

The antidote to first-rank poison is P-KR3 or P-KN3, to give the castled king "a little air." Lack of this precaution sometimes leads to unpleasant surprises, as in Diagram V-23. The position arises from the *Marshall Gambit* in the *Ruy Lopez*. It seems that Black will garner a whole rook from his impetuous attack, but White shows that there are always two kings to watch: 1 QxPch, RxQ 2 R-K8 mate.

V-24   **Black to Move**

A famous surprise move was sprung in Diagram V-24. White had massed pieces to gain a pawn. Black, while feigning to resist, had engineered a general exchange of minor pieces to steer into this position. White saw only that 1 . . . Q-N8ch 2 Q-B1, R-Q8? was not to be feared, for 3 R-B8ch would give him the victory. Hence White would have time (he believed) for P-KR3 or P-KN3. But Black played instead 1 . . . Q-N7! The first point is that 2 QxQ is out because of 2 . . . R-Q8 mate. The second point is that 2 Q-K1 to save both attacked pieces likewise fails to 2 . . . QxR 3 QxQ, R-Q8ch. The third point is that 2 R-B2 decoys the rook to a fatal square: 2 . . . Q-N8ch 3 Q-B1, QxR. Finally, 2 R-Q3 is obviously no good against 2 . . . Q-N8ch.

A beautiful example of maneuvering against overloaded heavy pieces is Diagram V-25. The Black queen must maintain guard of

V-25 **White to Move**

K1, or else White's RxRch will lead to mate. So, 1 Q-KN4! and the Black queen must look to her own safety. There followed 1 . . . Q-N4 2 Q-QB4, Q-Q2 (of course 2 . . . RxQ would be as fatal as QxQ) 3 Q-B7, Q-N4 4 P-QR4, QxRP 5 R-K4, Q-N4 (if 5 . . . RxR 6 QxRch; if 5 . . . QxR 6 RxQ, and Black cannot reply RxQ) 6 QxNP, Resigns, for the harried queen longer has a haven.

QUIZ V

In each of the following positions, the player whose turn it is to move can win. Show the winning combination.

1 White to move.

2 White to move.

3 White to move.

4 White to move.

5 White to move.

6 White to move.

7 White to move.

8 White moves 1 RxQ. Show how Black can now win.

9 Black to move.　　　**10** White to move.

ANSWERS TO QUIZ V

1. White mates in two:　1 Q-R6ch, KxQ 2 N(4)-B5.

2. White mates in three:　1 N-N6ch, NxN (or K-N1 2 R-N7 mate) 2 R-N8ch, N-B1 3 RxN.

3. White mates in two:　1 Q-B7ch, NxQ 2 N-K6.

4. 1 N-Q6ch, K-B1 2 Q-B6ch, PxQ 3 R-B7 mate. Black can last a little longer by 1 . . . QxN.

5. R-N6, PxR 2 QxNch, PxQ 3 BxP mate. If 1 . . . Q-B5, 2 RxN, and the rook is immune. The best that Black can do is to give up his queen for two pieces: 1 . . . QxR 2 BxQ, PxB.

6. White mates in four:　QxPch, KxQ 2 B-B5ch, K-K1 (if K-B3, 3 B-Q7 mate) 3 B-Q7ch, K-B1 or Q1 4 BxN.

7. 1 R-Q6, P-N3 2 RxQ, PxQ 3 BxPch, K-B1 4 B-R6 mate. Of course, if 1 . . . QxR, 2 QxBP is mate at once. Black can prolong the game only by giving up his queen for the rook, as by 1 . . . R-KB1 or N-N3.

8. 1 . . . B-N7ch 2 RxB (forced, for 2 K-N1, N-R6 would be mate), PxRch 2 K-N1, N-K7ch 3 KxP, NxQ. Black remains ahead by the exchange and a pawn—ample to win.

9. 1 . . . P-Q4. White has to leave his bishop to be taken, in order to make a defensive move such as N-N1, for, if 2 BxP or QxP, Black mates by 2 . . . QxPch 3 PxQ, B-R6.

10. 1 NxN, BxQ (if . . . PxN 2 QxB) 2 B-N5ch, K-K2 3 N-Q7, discovered check, mates next.

Lesson VI

MATING COMBINATIONS: PART TWO

In Lesson V we remarked that mating combinations fall into patterns according to the weaknesses on which they are based. In the present lesson we shall discuss various patterns of attack based on a faulty disposition of the pieces to protect the castled king. It is no coincidence that many of these combinations begin with sacrifices to smash up the pawns in front of the king.

TWO OPEN FILES

In Diagram VI-1, the absence of pieces from the Black K-side and the excellent positions of the White heavy pieces fairly scream

VI-1   **White to Move**

for a sacrifice to open the KN-file: 1 QxPch, KxQ 2 R-N1ch, K any 3 R-R3ch, Q-R5 4 RxQ mate.

VI-2   **White to Move**

Few mating combinations on two adjacent open files are so simple. Usually there are some defensive resources that only the queen can nullify. In Diagram VI-2, a like sacrifice is inviting: 1 RxPch, PxR 2 QxPch, K-R1. Now how shall White continue? A simple plan is 3 R-N1; White then threatens a fatal queen check on the KR-file as well as Q-N7 mate. Observe that, in all such positions, an interposition by Black at his KR2 is insufficient. 3 . . . R-B2 (with the idea that if 4 QxR, QxRch, and Black wins) 4 Q-R6ch, R-R2 5 Q-B6ch, R-N2 6 QxR mate. Likewise if 3 . . . Q-K2 4 Q-R5ch, Q-R2 5 Q-K5ch, etc. (White could also win by 3 R-K4, threatening R-R4, but this line requires more calculation.)

VI-3   **White to Move**

In Diagram VI-3, White would, of course, like to play PxP, opening the file for his rook, but this queen sacrifice does not seem to be quite adequate: e.g., 1 PxP, QxQ 2 RxPch, K-B1 3 P-R7, K-K2. But a different sacrifice of the queen pays off: 1 QxP! PxQ 2 PxPch, K-B1.   Now, if 3 P-R7, Black can reply Q-R5, give up his queen for the passed pawn, and win one of the White bishops (both of which are loose).   But White has a vital tempo-saving device akin to that pointed out in Diagram V-16.   He sacrifices his rook to advance the passed pawn without loss of time: 3 R-N8ch! KxR 4 P-R7ch, K-B1 5 P-R8 (Q) mate.

THE OPEN KN-FILE

The sacrificial opening of the KN-file precedes several routine combinations in which mate is effected by a queen and a rook or by

VI-4   **Black to Move**

a queen and a bishop. Diagram VI-4 is much like preceding examples, in which the absence of pieces from the assailed White K-side invites strong-arm tactics: 1 . . . RxPch 2 KxR, Q-N3ch 3 K-R1 (not 3 K-B3, Q-N5 mate), B-Q4ch 4 P-B3. Now the sole piece defending the hapless king is overloaded, so: 4 . . . BxPch 5 RxB, Q-N8 mate.

VI-5   **White to Move**

A beautiful example showing a medley of tactical ideas is Diagram VI-5. Black has just made the natural-looking move of R(KB1)-K1, challenging the file. White has invited this move, for he is ready with a deep combination. The first step is 1 Q-N5! threatening mate at Black's KN2, and, of course, 1 . . . QxQ allows 2 RxR mate. Black is forced to move 1 . . . P-KN3. Then 2 Q-R6 again threatens Q-N7, so that 2 . . . PxN is forced. Now that the KN-file is open, White uses it as a lever to force open the diagonal for his bishop, 3 R-N4ch! PxR. The finish is a familiar queen-bishop maneuver based on the absence of any guard for Black's KB2: 4 BxPch (in such positions, QxPch is a mistake, for the enemy king then escapes via B1 and K2), K-R1 5 B-N6ch, K-N1 6 Q-R7ch, K-B1 7 QxP mate.

VI-6   **White to Move**

When the rook still stands on KB1 after O-O, blocking the king, the removal of the KNP may allow a mate by rook and bishop—the queen is not needed. The typical finish occurred in Diagram VI-6. Here Black seems well poised for defense: his KN is at his strongest defensive post, KB3, and the queen is nearby. But White enjoys several positional advantages: the open file for his KR and the *fianchettoed* (developed on the flank) bishop bearing on the enemy K-side. He unmasks the latter with devastating effect: 1 NxP! PxN (not 1 . . . NxN 2 QxP mate, while after 1 . . . N-K1 or any other defense White has both an extra pawn and a powerful attack) 2 QxN! PxQ 3 R-N1ch, K-R1 4 BxP mate.

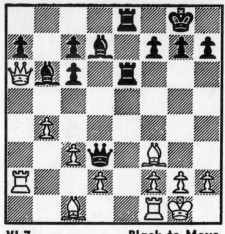

VI-7   **Black to Move**

A famous demonstration of the force of a queenless attack through an open KN-file was given by Paul Morphy and is illustrated in Diagram VI-7. Black played 1 . . . QxB! 2 PxQ, R-N3ch 3 K-R1, B-R6. This move threatens B-N7ch followed by BxP mate. The only possible defense is to move the rook to give the king a flight. (4 R-N1 is no good because of 4 . . .′. B-N7ch 5 RxB, R-K8ch and mate in two.) So: 4 R-Q1, B-N7ch 5 K-N1, BxPch 6 K-B1, B-N7ch 7 K-N1, B-R6ch 8 K-R1. Having picked off a pawn in anticipation of the coming endgame, Black now proceeds to get his queen back: 8 . . . BxP. To stop mate, White has to play 9 Q-B1, and BxQ leaves Black with a decisive material superiority. (He actually won quickly by threat of mate, the White bishop and QR being unable to reach the K-side in time.)

THE OPEN KR-FILE

A large group of combinations is typified by Diagram VI-8. Black has left *holes* in front of his castled king by advancing his KN

VI-8   **White to Move**

pawn. His KB does not stand on KN2 to protect these holes. White
has consequently been able to post a bishop at his KB6, so that he can
mate if he can maneuver his queen to KN7 or KR8. The avenue of
entry is the diagonal leading to his KR6, and Black has just interposed
on this diagonal with N-B5ch. But White's rooks have reached the
crucial KR-file, so that White no longer needs his queen. 1 QxN!
BxQ 2 RxP, PxR 3 RxP, and Black resigns, since mate by R-R8 is
inevitable.

VI-9   **White to Move**

With this rook-and-bishop mate in mind, we can see that, after P-KN3 creates the *holes* on which the mate is based, the pawn at KR2 may in effect be overloaded in attempting to keep the KR-file closed and at the same time to guard KN3. This overload is the basis of many sacrificial captures on the enemy's KN3. An instance is Diagram VI-9. White plays 1 BxP, smashing through the pawn barrier. Black cannot answer 1 . . . RPxB because of 2 R-R8 mate, nor 1 . . . BPxB because of 2 QxN mate. If 1 . . . NxB, 2 RxNch, and again Black finds both his pawns pinned: 2 . . . BPxR 3 Q-B8 mate or 2 . . . RPxR, 3 R-R4 and 4 R-R8 mate. Since Black cannot capture the saucy bishop, he is constrained to strengthen his defense against a fierce attack heightened by the White bishop's access to his KR7. Subsequent analysis of this historic game uncovered the main variation: 1 . . . R-N3 2 N-K6 (a tremendous obstructive move), QRxN! 3 BxRPch, NxB 4 R-N4ch. This move takes advantage of the obstruction of Black's QB, who could otherwise capture the rook. But observe that 2 . . . BxN obstructing the QR would give White a vital tempo, by momentarily parrying the attack on his queen, to commit slaughter by 3 BxRPch, NxB 4 RxN, KxR 5 R-R4ch, K-N1 6 R-R8 mate—the "thematic" mate. So, to return to the analyzed line: 4 R-N4ch, K-B1 5 Q-R8 mate.

BISHOP SACRIFICE AT KR7

The strongest single piece for the defense of the castled king is a knight at B3. After O-O, the knight at KB3 guards the RP, shields the KBP from frontal attack, and, above all, prevents enemy pieces from occupying KR4 and KN5 unchallenged. The withdrawal of this knight, when the enemy has any considerable force bearing on the K-side, invites a sacrificial attack. In a sense, the particular piece or square of sacrifice is accidental—any K-side pawn is worth the piece that happens to bear on it at this juncture.

VI-10   **White to Move**

A modern instance is Diagram VI-10. White has the classic development of two bishops bearing on the Black K-side, his KN ready to go to N5, and his queen ready to sally forth to KR5 or KN4. Black has impaired his defensive posture by removing his knight from KB3. The sacrifice 1 BxPch has been the subject of analysis since the earliest days of historical chess. Here the soundness of the sacrifice is relatively easy to demonstrate.

After 1 BxPch, KxB 2 N-N5ch, K-N1 3 Q-R5, White threatens, above all, QxPch, forcing the king onto the open KR-file, after which R-K4 with threat of R-R4ch is unanswerable. But any effort by Black to guard his KB2 (by R-KB1, R-K2, or Q-K2) blocks a vital flight square for the king and allows a mate by 4 Q-R7ch, etc. Therefore White's 2 N-N5ch draws the Black king into the open: 2 . . . K-N3. Now, as White may well judge, the exposed situation of the king will enable White either to mate or to win material in excess of what he has sacrificed. In fact, there are several roads to either goal. The actual continuation was 3 P-KR4, R-R1 4 RxPch, N-B3 (since 4 . . . PxR 5 Q-Q3ch would be murderous) 5 P-R5ch, K-R3 6 RxB, Resigns.

TWO BISHOPS SACRIFICE

In similar circumstances—the enemy K-side denuded of defending pieces—a player may be able to sacrifice both his bishops to re-

VI-11   **Black to Move**

move the enemy KRP and KNP, opening the way for a smashing attack on the files. Diagram VI-11 repeats in all essentials a combination that was demonstrated many years earlier, 1 . . . P-Q5 (merely to open the line for the QB, but incidentally threatening to win a pawn on his K6) 2 PxP? (the only hope was a defensive move such as N-B3, letting the pawn go), BxPch! 3 KxB, Q-R5ch 4 K-N1, BxP! This threatens Q-R8 mate, but 5 KxB fails against 5 . . . Q-N5ch 6 K-R1, R-Q4 with threat of R-R4 mate. Hence White can but provide a flight, 4 P-B3. There followed 4 . . . KR-K1 5 N-K4, Q-R8ch 6 K-B2, BxR with material gain, since 7 RxB is met by Q-R7ch and QxQ. Black threatens Q-N7ch and QxQ, swapping off to win by his material advantage; White therefore has no time to capitalize on the momentary pin of Black's bishop.

OVERLOADED PAWNS

One conclusion that we may draw from the foregoing examples is that the defensive K-side pawns after O-O may find themselves overloaded if the enemy has a superior force bearing on that side. Enemy pieces settle with impunity on the third-rank squares guarded by the pawns, since a pawn capture may open a line fatally. A beauti-

VI-12   **Black to Move**

ful illustration is Diagram VI-12, for a game played *rapid transit* at ten seconds per move. White seems to have weathered the light-horse attack: e.g., 1 . . . NxNP 2 Q-B3, BxN 3 P-B3 and wins back his piece; or 1 . . . BxP 2 BxN, BxR 3 QxB. But Black puts his finger on the weakness of the White position: 1 . . . Q-R6! This threatens QxNP mate, and the capture of either minor piece is no answer. If 2 PxQ, the opening of the diagonal for the bishop is fatal: 2 . . . NxP mate.

VI-13   **Black to Move**

One of the most celebrated moves of this kind was made in Diagram VI-13. Black has just captured a bishop at his KR6—not an offer of an exchange, since PxR would be met by N-B6ch winning the queen. White has replied by R(K5)-B5 with the idea that after the Black queen moves he will continue R-B7 with threat of mate and prospect of getting his queen off the square KN5 without loss of time, so as then to be able to play PxR in safety. But Marshall, the American champion, crosses up Black's rosy ideas with the extraordinary move 1 . . . Q-KN6! The story goes that the spectators showered the chessboard with gold pieces in appreciation of this beautiful riposte.

When he realized the consequences of this move, White resigned. Since the queen threatens to take the RP with mate, she must be captured. But 2 BPxQ fails against 2 . . . N-K7ch 3 K-R1, RxR mate. Even worse is 2 RPxQ, N-K7 mate. If 2 QxQ, then 2 . . . N-K7ch 3 K-R1, NxQch 4 K-N1, NxR, and Black emerges a piece ahead.

VI-14   **White to Move**

With this prototype before us, we can readily understand why a player will as a matter of course examine the move Q-N6 in the teeth of two pawns—and occasionally find that it works. In Diagram VI-14, we see that 1 Q-N6 is forceful, since it threatens both QxNP mate and QxRPch followed by R-R3 mate. Black thus can find no defense but to capture the queen. Obviously 1 . . . RPxQ allows 2 R-R3 mate, while 1 . . . BPxQ opens the diagonal of the bishop to leave the Black king stalemated. Can White capitalize on this fact? Yes, by 2 NxPch, PxN 3 R-R3 mate.

VI-15   **White to Move**

We interject here another example of the pattern move N-N6ch to open the enemy's KR-file. In Diagram VI-15 Black has just captured a bishop at his KN6, counting perhaps only on 1 RPxN, K-R1, and on thus gaining a breathing spell to bolster his defense. But the thunderbolt strikes too quickly: 1 N-K7ch, K-R1 2 N-N6ch, PxN 3 RPxNch with mate to follow.

VI-16   **White to Move**

To return to the queen-sacrifice at KN6, Diagram VI-16 is a more intricate example than the foregoing. By analogy, 1 QxN looks inviting, but does it work in all variations? We see that 1 . . . BPxQ 2 BxPch finds Black singularly unprepared to make an effective interposition, so that after 2 . . . K-R1 3 NxP is mate. But what about 1 . . . RPxQ? Well, the KR-file is opened for the White rook; this circumstance helps to uncover the winning continuation: 2 NxP (threat R-R8 mate), PxN 3 BxPch, K-B1 4 R-R8 mate.

QUIZ VI

1 White to move and mate in four.

2 White moves 1 N-Q7. Show how this move wins.

3 Black to move and win.

4 White to move and win.

5 White to move and win.

6 White can win a pawn quickly. How?

7 White to move. How can he most quickly capitalize on his advantage?

8 How should White continue his attack?

9 What is White's best move? How should he follow it up?

10 Black to move. (See question below.)

10 (a) What is the correct general plan for Black? (b) What should be his first move to further that plan?

ANSWERS TO QUIZ VI

1. 1 QxRPch, K-N1 2 Q-R8ch, KxQ 3 BxPch, K-N1 4 R-R8 mate.

2. To capture the knight would cost Black material: 1 . . . QxN 2 BxPch, KxB 3 RxQ, NxR 4 Q-Q3ch, K-N1 5 QxN. Therefore Black has to move his KR to keep from losing the exchange. White continues 2 BxN, PxB 3 Q-N4ch, K-R1 4 Q-R4 (threat QxRP mate), P-B4 5 N-B6, and Black must give up his queen for the knight to escape mate. (Useless is 5 . . . K-N2 6 Q-N5ch, K-R1 7 Q-R6.)

3. 1 . . . QxR! 2 PxQ, B-B4ch 3 Q-B2 (not 3 K-B1, R-R8 mate). Now Black could liquidate and gain the exchange by BxQch, but he has a better plan: 3 . . . R-R8ch! 4 KxR, BxQ, and White cannot prevent R-R1 mate next move.

4. 1 RxN, KxR (if BxR 2 QxP, R-B1 3 R-Q1 and mate soon) 2 Q-Q1ch, K-B2 3 Q-Q8ch, K-N1 4 R-Q1. The threat is 5 R-Q7 and 6 Q-B7 mate. Black can escape only at ruinous cost (e.g., 4 . . . BxP 5 QxR, B-N3). The actual finish was 4 . . . P-B3 5 R-Q7, P-QR3 6 RxPch, KxR 7 Q-N6 mate.

5. 1 N-B6ch, PxN 2 R-N1ch, K-R1 3 QxPch, NxQ 4 BxP mate. If 1 . . . NxN, 2 QxN with the same outcome.

6. 1 B-K4. Black has no way to guard his QNP. His QR cannot defend it, since the rook is tied to the 1st rank to prevent R-Q8 mate. The knight has no square of withdrawal to open the file for guard by the other rook.

7. 1 KRxN! Black cannot reply QxR, for then 2 N-K4, and there is no time to save the queen because of the threat of 3 R-R8 mate. Therefore, 1 . . . PxR 2 N-Q5! The knight wants to reach KB6, with threat of Q-R7 mate. Good enough would be 2 N-K4, but N-Q5 is more forceful because it attacks the queen. That the knight can be captured does not matter, for the line openings will then be fatal—but Black did play 2 . . . PxN. Then 3 Q-R7ch! KxQ 4 R-R6ch, K-N1 5 R-R8 mate.

8. 1 B-B6, threatening 2 Q-N5 or even 2 BxNP. Fatal is 1 . . . P-N3 2 Q-R6. If 1 . . . KR-K1 (to let the KB retreat to B1),

a possible line is 2 N-N5, P-R3 3 BxNP, KxB 4 NxBch, PxN 5 Q-B6ch, K-R2 6 BxP. The main variation is 1 . . . PxB 2 N-N5! (the sacrifice of the second piece is essential to allow Q-B6 with check, denying Black a tempo for defense), PxN 3 QxNPch, K-R1 4 Q-B6ch, K-N1 5 R-B3. Now Black's one tempo for a defensive move is insufficient. The actual continuation was 5 . . . KR-K1 (to give the king a flight) 6 Q-R6 (killing the flight), B-N5 7 R-N3, Q-Q2 8 Q-N5ch, and presently RxB forcing Black to give up his queen for the rook to escape mate.

9. 1 P-B5! The White heavy pieces are well posted for a mating attack, and the Black pieces are badly posted for defense. White can afford to sacrifice his knight to open a file. If 1 . . . KPxP 2 NxP! PxN, White might continue 3 Q-N5ch, K-R2 (not Q-N3 4 QxRch) 4 RxP with decisive penetration. Even stronger is 3 RxP first (3 . . . Q-N3? 4 R-N5). If Black does not capture the BP (he did not), then White exchanges pawns to open the KB-file and goes to work on it with his rooks (1 . . . R-R2 2 PxNP, PxP 3 R-B6). We can readily see that, even if Black can avoid mate, he cannot save all his backward pawns. (3 . . . Q-Q1 4 Q-R2, R-K2 5 P-Q5, etc.)

10. (a) Black has much the greater space on the K-side. His correct plan is to mass pieces there for a mating attack. Sooner or later he must open a file for infiltration. If White leaves his K-side pawns unmoved, Black can open a file by moving P-KN4-N5, supported, if need be, by P-KR4. As a rule, he should dispose his pieces to take advantage of the line opening, before moving P-N5, say by K-R1, R-KN1, B-KR3, etc.

(b) Black should begin with 1 . . . P-KN4. This maintains the bind against various efforts to break loose: e.g., the sacrifice of a piece for two pawns on White's KB4. White actually tried 2 P-KN4, PxPe.p. 3 RPxP, P-KR3, and Black's KNP is seen to perform the important service of preventing White from moving P-KB4 and from gaining space for his pieces.

Lesson VII

STRATEGICAL OBJECTIVES: PART ONE

The ultimate objective in chess is, of course, to checkmate the enemy king. Now, the mating combinations such as those shown in the two preceding lessons can arise only when one side has a marked advantage in position or material. Such superiority may spring from a single blunder by the opponent in an even game but much more often grows by an accumulation of small advantages. At all events, you cannot count upon an opponent's blunder to give you the victory! You must bend your energies to gaining small advantages, step by step.

Without forgetting the ultimate objective, you must set your sights on a whole series of limited ones. At all times keep in mind these general objectives:

To gain control of the center.

To develop rapidly and effectively.

To increase your space for maneuver.

To avoid organic pawn weakness.

To assure the safety of your king.

Other objectives may arise from particular positions. Chief of these are:

To establish an outpost.

To open a file for your rooks.

To seize and hold an open file.

To mobilize a pawn wing.

To win the "minor exchange."

We will now discuss each item on the foregoing lists.

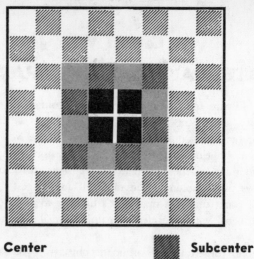

Center   **Subcenter**

In a narrow sense, the center comprises the four squares: K4, K5, Q4, Q5. The importance of the center is that pieces posted here have their maximum range of action. Thus, a bishop at Q4 hits at both enemy wings; a knight at K5 strikes at the heart of the enemy camp. From the very first move, bear in mind the urgency of *excluding enemy pieces from the center.*

VII-1   **White Phalanx Versus Black Chain**

The simplest way to achieve this objective is to advance your center pawns—and maintain them. Most games begin 1 P-K4 or 1 P-Q4 for this purpose.* The ideal offensive formation is the *phalanx,* or two pawns abreast, as the White pawns in Diagram VII-1. These pawns exclude enemy pieces from four central squares of the enemy's rank and can be heavily guarded by pieces and pawns to prevent their capture (i.e., enemy occupation of his 5th rank).

White, because he has the first move, usually can set up a center phalanx if he pleases, whereas Black usually can do no more than establish a defensive *chain* (Black pawns in Diagram VII-1). White has the obvious advantage that both his bishops can develop toward the center, whereas the Black 3rd-rank pawn blocks one of his own bishops. Also, White has the option of PxP or P-K5, whereas Black can change the center constellation only by PxP (disregarding for the moment the *subcenter* pawns on the bishop files). This exchange by Black leaves White with the greater central space and also does not solve the problem of how Black is to get his QB into action.

A number of the regular openings begin with a bid by White to establish the center phalanx:

    Center Game: 1 P-K4, P-K4 2 P-Q4

    Scotch Game: 1 P-K4, P-K4 2 N-KB3, N-QB3 3 P-Q4

In both cases Black is compelled to play PxP but can soon equalize by enforcing P-Q4.

If Black begins by committing himself to a chain, White does best to form the phalanx immediately:

    French Defense: 1 P-K4, P-K3 2 P-Q4

    Caro-Kann Defense: 1 P-K4, P-QB3 2 P-Q4

    Philidor's Defense: 1 P-K4, P-K4 2 N-KB3, P-Q3 3 P-Q4

In some regular openings, White maintains his phalanx versus chain by bringing up the bishop to guard his attacked center pawn.

---

*In modern play, center pawn advances are often delayed until two or three minor pieces have been developed to support theem. Such refinements are outside the province of this lesson. It remains true that the K-pawn and Q-pawn must advance sooner or later to dispute control of the center.

Giuoco Piano: 1 P-K4, P-K4 2 N-KB3, N-QB3 3 B-B4, B-B4 4 P-B3 (Diagram VII-2). White intends 5 P-Q4 and makes this

VII-2   **Giuoco Piano**

move even after 4 . . . N-B3. (Black can then win a pawn by 5 . . . PxP 6 PxP, B-N5ch 7 N-B3, NxKP, but after 8 O-O White has ample compensation in his superior development.)

White may form a phalanx across the subcenter:

    King's Gambit*:   1 P-K4, P-K4 2 P-KB4
    Queen's Gambit: 1 P-Q4, P-Q4 2 P-QB4

In such cases, PxP by Black is not so good for him as it is in the *Center Game* and the *Scotch Game,* because here he gives up a center pawn for a wing pawn. White's two-pawns-to-one then gives him the better prospect for gaining center control.

Black may advance a wing pawn at his first turn to oppose the formation of a White center phalanx:

    Sicilian Defense: 1 P-K4, P-QB4
    Dutch Defense: 1 P-Q4, P-KB4

In the *Sicilian,* White can enforce P-Q4 and usually does so at once by 2 N-KB3 and 3 P-Q4 before Black can mass his pieces to prevent the advance. Then after 3 . . . PxP it is Black who has two pawns

---

*A gambit is the offer, usually of a pawn, for positional advantage. In former times the name was applied loosely and often inaccurately: e.g., the *Queen's Gambit* is not an actual sacrifice. In modern times, usage has gone to the other extreme; one reads of the "Marshall Variation" in the *Ruy Lopez,* although it is a true gambit.

to one in the center—but he cannot advance them for a long time, and White quickly obtains greater space to maneuver. In the *Dutch Defense*, White cannot enforce P-K4 without extensive preparation—but neither can Black. Black suffers a central cramp, to relieve which he may have to accept an organic pawn weakness.

If the center pawns disappear early, control of the center by pieces becomes paramount. A marked superiority here may be decisive, as the following game shows.

CARO-KANN DEFENSE

1 P-K4	P-QB3	4 NxP	N-B3
2 P-Q4	P-Q4	5 N-N3	P-K3
3 N-QB3	PxP	6 N-B3	P-B4

The idea of the defense is now seen. Black dissolves the center pawns to gain free development for his pieces.

7 B-Q3

Not 7 PxP, QxQch 8 KxQ, BxP, and Black has the better game. White shields his queen to be able to play PxP. Black cannot now win the QP: 7 . . . PxP 8 NxP, QxN?? 8 B-N5ch.

7 . . .	N-B3	10 O-O	P-QN3
8 PxP	BxP	11 P-N4	B-K2
9 P-QR3	O-O	12 B-N2	Q-B2

VII-3   **After 12 . . . Q-B2**

Of the four center squares, Black controls only his Q4. The natural use of this square is as a post for his KN, yet White can nullify this post by P-QB4 and—more important—Black needs his knight on B3 to defend his king. By his next move White obtains the post K5 for his own KN.

13 P-N5	N-QR4

As a direct consequence of White's great center control, the Black pieces are so huddled that his KB stands on the square to which the knight might otherwise retreat to remain centralized. Instead, the knight must go into limbo on the Q-side.

14 N-K5	B-N2
15 N-N4	

Having both his bishops trained on the Black K-side, White wants to swap off Black's KN. Black finds the best defense, after which 16 NxNch would lead to exchanges easing his situation.

15 . . .	Q-Q1
16 N-K3	

"Retreating, the better to advance." (Comment by former world champion Dr. Euwe.)

16 . . .	N-Q4

Black hopes to enforce some exchanges anyway, but he is frustrated. The removal of the knight from KB3, in the face of the enemy bishops, should always be regarded with suspicion.

17 Q-R5	P-N3

Forced. Of course, N-KB3 loses to 18 BxN, and P-KR3 loses to 18 BxP, KxB 19 N-B5ch, etc. But now Black has opened *holes* on his K-side that prove fatal.

18 N-N4!	

Threatening N-R6 mate. Now Black has to interpose his bishop and lose it for a knight, leaving his dark squares very weak, since 18 . . . N-B3 19 Q-K5 leaves him hopelessly tied up. (19 . . . Q-Q4 threatens mate but loses a piece by 20 QxQ.) Nor can he survive after 18 . . . P-B3 19 KBxP, PxB 20 QxPch.

18 . . .	B-B3	20 Q-R6	QR-B1
19 NxBch	NxN	21 QR-Q1	Q-K2
22 KR-K1			

Now White threatens 23 N-B5.

22 . . .	N-K1	24 R-K5	B-Q4
23 N-B5	Q-B4	25 N-K7ch	Resigns

Not waiting for 25 . . . QxN 26 QxPch, KxQ 27 R-R5ch and 28 R-R8 mate.

DEVELOPMENT

Developing a piece means moving it from its initial post, usually to a post off the back row. (A rook may be developed by being moved on the back row to an open file or to back up an advanced pawn.) Development as a whole is the process of bringing all your pieces into action. This first stage of a game may be considered ended when you have gotten your knights, bishops, and queen off the back row and have castled or otherwise connected your rooks. In a larger sense, development is the disposition of your pieces at any stage, right down to an end game.

In the opening, bear in mind these objectives:

(a) Make only as many pawn moves as are necessary to gain a fair share of center control and to assure good posts for your pieces.

(b) Develop each piece so that it either reinforces your center control or hits at a weak spot in the enemy camp.

(c) Avoid the loss of time that results from putting a piece on a square from which it can be forced to retreat by an enemy's developing move.

(d) Hamper and restrict the enemy's development when a reasonable opportunity is offered.

(e) Complete your development before attempting to smash through the enemy lines; refrain from lighthorse attacks with insufficient means.

There are some ancient maxims about development: "Bring out knights before bishops"; "Never move a piece twice in the opening until you have moved each piece once." Unfortunately, such generalities are usually false. It is scarcely possible to give sound general advice. We shall therefore give examples of unsound opening play, illustrating certain common errors.

The Superfluous Pawn Move. Some pawn moves in the opening are unavoidable. But every pawn move represents a lost opportunity to develop a piece. Beware, therefore, of superfluous pawn moves. A famous instance of the punishment that can follow disregard of this caution is:

1 P-Q4	P-Q4	3 P-B4	BPxP
2 N-KB3	P-QB4	4 PxP	N-KB3
	5 NxP		P-QR3?

VII-4   After 5 . . . P-QR3?

Why? There is nothing to be feared from 5 . . . NxP 6 N-N5,
with the transparent threat of QxN; 6 . . . P-K3 is a sufficient reply.

6 P-K4!

The QP cramps Black's development. White sees a way to maintain it by giving up his KP instead (which Black has to take, or else
he remains a pawn down).

6 . . .   NxKP
7 Q-R4ch   B-Q2

Black blocks his own queen, but no other reply was feasible:
7 . . . Q-Q2 loses to 8 B-QN5, and 7 . . . P-QN4 loses to 8 BxPch.

8 Q-N3

Having pulled the Black QB from protection of QNP, White
gains a tempo by attacking the bishop. Black does not defend by
8 . . . Q-B2, because a White rook would soon come to the QB-file
and chase the queen away. His actual move looks good, because it
regains the tempo by attacking the queen and also brings the knight
back from his untenable position in "left field."

8 . . .   N-B4
9 Q-K3   P-KN3

How else is Black to continue his development? He does not
relish P-K3, which at the least would give him an isolated KP.

10 N-KB3

Developing backward, yet with no loss of time, because the Black knight is attacked. Since the knight has no good retreat and P-K3 would now be worse, the knight must be defended where he stands.

$$10 \ldots \qquad\qquad \text{Q-B2}$$
$$11 \ \text{Q-B3} \qquad\qquad \text{R-N1}$$

Not 11 . . . P-B3 to retain the possibility of O-O, for after 12 B-K3 Black would be in serious trouble.

VII-5 **After 11 . . . R-N1**

Now look at the dreary prospect ahead for Black. He can never play O-O. He cannot continue developing without incurring some further disruption of his pawn skeleton. Two of his developed pieces (queen and KN) are in jeopardy because they stand on an open file.

White has achieved this position by four pawn moves, four moves of the queen, and three by the knight. So much for the maxim, "Never move a piece twice." But we are bound to point out that such repeated moves of the same pieces cannot be good except to capitalize on a very bad move by the enemy.

The Lighthorse Attack. Undoubtedly one of your very first chess games went like this (you were Black) : 1 P-K4, P-K4 2 B-B4, B-B4 3 Q-R5, N-KB3 4 QxP mate. Of course, this *Scholar's Mate* is easily parried (if you notice that it is threatened) by 3 . . . Q-K2; then you can chase the queen by the developing move N-KB3, and White has forfeited his advantage of the first move.

In the initial position of the chess pieces, KB2 is the weakest spot in the player's camp. The temptation to mount a lighthorse attack against it is irresistible to novices—and sometimes to masters! Unfortunately, we cannot dismiss all such attacks as lighthorse. In the *Two Knights Defense* (1 P-K4, P-K4 2 N-KB3, N-QB3 3 B-B4, N-B3), the *Prussian Attack* 4 N-N5 has been "refuted" and "rehabilitated" repeatedly in chess history. Despite more analysis than has been expended on any other opening, no one can yet say whether the attack is sound or unsound.

In the following game (played almost 100 years ago), however, an experienced player might well judge from certain stigmata that the attack was doomed to failure.

GIUOCO PIANO

1 P-K4	P-K4	4 P-B3	N-B3
2 N-KB3	N-QB3	5 P-QN4	B-N3
3 B-B4	B-B4	6 Q-N3	

The object of White's 5th move was to forestall 6 . . . N-QR4.

| 6 . . . | O-O |
| 7 N-N5 | |

VII-6   **After 7 N-N5**

Here it is: the attack on the KBP. Can it succeed? A seasoned player would argue: Black has developed his three minor pieces on their most natural posts and has castled. White has had to develop unnaturally to mount this attack and has given a tempo (by two moves of the knight). If this attack is any good, then we have to revise our whole theory of the opening and concentrate from the first move on defense of the KBP. Not likely!

| 7 . . . | BxPch! |

Demonstrating that Black is better poised for attack than White! If 8 KxB, N-N5ch and 9 . . . QxN, smashing the White attack and winning a pawn.

| 8 K-B1 | B-N3 |
| 9 NxBP | |

If White does not take the pawn, he has nothing to show for his material deficit and miserable position.

| 9 . . . | NxKP! |

Pinning the knight and once more winning a pawn. If you now wonder why White did not move 8 K-K2 or Q1 to avoid this pin, ponder the consequences of 8 . . . P-Q4 9 BxP, B-N5ch.

| 10 K-K2 | Q-R5 |

The discovered check can do Black no harm. Nor can White draw by repetition: 11 N-R6ch, K-R1 12 N-B7ch, for Black's lead allows 12 . . . RxN.

| 11 R-B1 | N-B7 |

Squelching White's threat of 12 N-R6ch, K-R1 13 RxR mate. Now Black threatens mate in one—and he always has P-Q4 followed by B-N5ch in reserve.

| 12 NxPch | K-R1 | 14 N-Q2 | BxP! |
| 13 P-Q4 | BxP | 15 QxB | |

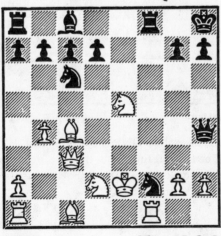

VII-7   **After 15 QxB**

Black has set the stage for a combinative windup.

15 . . .	N-Q5ch	17 K-Q1	Q-K8ch
16 K-K1	N-Q6ch	18 RxQ	N-B7 mate

Pawn-Grabbing. There is a legend that a dying man said to his son, "My boy, I have no worldly wealth, but I have one pearl of wisdom to bequeath to you: don't take the queen's knight's pawn!" The following game illustrates the value of this counsel.

CENTER COUNTER GAMBIT

1 P-K4		P-Q4
2 PxP		P-QB3

Offering a real gambit, which White spurns.

3 P-Q4	PxP	6 N-KB3	B-N5
4 B-Q3	N-QB3	7 P-KR3	BxN
5 B-K3	N-B3	8 QxB	Q-N3
9 O-O			

VII-8   **After 9 O-O**

The case for taking the QNP is of course that "a pawn is a pawn is a pawn." The case against it is that the marauding queen loses time and may get into jeopardy. Here the pawn is particularly tempting because Black can also win the QP.

9 . . .	QxNP	12 Q-R4ch	N-Q2
10 N-Q2	NxP	13 QR-N1	Q-B6
11 Q-B4	N-K3	14 RxP	N-B2

14 . . . R-Q1 is no better. For example, 15 B-QN5, N-B2 16 BxNch, RxB 16 R-N8 mate.

15 B-Q4	QxN	17 QxNch	RxQ
16 RxN	R-Q1	18 R-B8ch	R-Q1
	19 B-N5 mate		

Irrelevant Development. We once met a player who had a theory of the opening based on "ideal formations." So we played him a game to let him demonstrate his stuff. He duly achieved one of his "ideal formations," and three moves later he was mated. The moral is, of course, that you cannot ignore what your opponent is doing. Any preconceived plan must be modified to meet the exigencies of the situation. This means more than parrying the one- and two-move threats: it means perceiving the *positional* threats inherent in the enemy's deployment and directing your own so as to avert or mitigate them.

Consider the following game.

BISHOP'S OPENING

1 P-K4	P-K4	3 P-Q4	PxP
2 B-B4	N-KB3	4 QxP	N-B3
	5 Q-K3		

VII-9   **After 5 Q-K3**

White has given away a tempo in development. In compensation, he has a center pawn on the 4th rank, and Black must constantly reckon with its advance. White cannot be prevented from moving P-KB4 eventually, to support P-K5 or to launch a K-side pawn storm.

A reasonable plan of development for Black is P-Q3 (to hold back the KP) and B-K3 (to challenge the powerful White KB). This will relegate the KB to K2—but he is wanted there anyhow, at first to preclude sacrificial attacks based on opening the K-file and later to neutralize a possible B-KN5 by White. The pin of the KN is a real menace whenever there is a possibility of enforcing P-K5.

Black might even start with 5 . . . B-K2, since this would threaten the freeing move 6 . . . P-Q4.

5 . . . .   P-QN3?

What is this? Is Black going to fianchetto his QB? Absurd! The bishop is needed in the center.

6 N-QB3   B-B4

The purpose is revealed—and a sorry one. Black chases the queen where she wants to go, at the same time opening the line for her own QB, while the Black KB forsakes the defense of the K-side.

7 Q-N3   O-O
8 B-KN5

There it is, the ominous pin! Black should now admit his previous error, move B-K2, then, if feasible, N-K1.

8 . . .   R-K1

Parries the immediate threat of P-K5, but obviously is useless as soon as White gets in P-KB4.

9 O-O-O   N-QR4

To drive away the dangerous bishop—who cheerfully retires to take up a new strong post, while the Black knight is left in limbo. Of course, 9 . . . N-K4 would have been even worse, for then White's P-KB4 would come in with the gain of a tempo.

10 B-K2   B-K2

The threat of P-K5 compels the move that Black should have made long ago.

11 P-B4   B-N2

Consistent but futile. However, P-Q3 would now cost him at least a pawn after 12 P-K5.

12 B-B3   K-R1

Clearing the square for N-N1, the rook having unwisely preempted K1.

13 P-KR4

Obviously intending to leave his QB to be captured, after, e.g., 13 . . . N-N1 and 14 . . . P-KB3, since the opening of the KR-file would be murderous.

13 . . .		P-B4	
14 KN-K2		QR-B1	

VII-10   **After 14 . . . QR-B1**

Black's last two moves, like the flowers that bloom in the spring, have nothing to do with the case. Relevant would be Q-B1, with the idea of bringing the QN to the K-side via B3, Q1, K3, or with the idea of P-Q3, N-Q2, P-KB3, N-B1. However, White could cross up these plans. Black's game is past redemption; now comes his execution.

15 P-K5	N-N1	24 QxNP	R-K2
16 KBxB	NxB	25 P-B6	Q-K1
17 P-B5	P-B3	26 P-B7	Q-B1
18 P-K6	P-Q3	27 RxBch	PxR
19 N-B4	PxB	28 R-R1	RxKP
20 N-N6ch	PxN	29 QxR	K-R2
21 PxPch	N-R3	30 N-K4	R-B2
22 PxN	B-N4ch	31 N-N5ch	K-R1
23 K-N1	BxP	32 RxPch	QxR
		33 QxQ mate	

SPACE

Until the center pawns are dissolved, the deployment of your pieces is restricted by your own pawn front. If the front is not sufficiently advanced, you may find yourself with too little interior space to permit an effective grouping of pieces to enforce their advance, or even to defend your king. Such a cramp may in itself result in defeat.

The most common source of a cramp is the center chain opposed to the phalanx or its frequent aftermath, the center pawn on the 3rd rank versus a pawn on the 4th. The following game is typical of thousands in which Black (who here was world champion Steinitz) fails to solve his perennial problem.

THREE KNIGHTS OPENING

1 P-K4	P-K4	4 P-Q4	PxP
2 N-KB3	N-QB3	5 NxP	B-N2
3 N-B3	P-KN3	6 B-K3	

VII-11   **After 6 B-K3**

So far all is "book." Modern analysis now prefers 6 . . . KN-K2. Black tries a different plan, which looks plausible.

6 . . .	N-B3	9 B-B3	P-Q3
7 B-K2	O-O	10 Q-Q2	N-Q2
8 O-O	N-K2	11 B-R6	N-K4
	12 BxB		KxB

Black is playing for a win; otherwise he would interpolate NxBch. It is remarkable how White keeps the upper hand despite the exchange of minor pieces.

13 B-K2	P-KB3
14 P-B4	

As often happens, a small superiority in space can be increased by "expansion" that the opponent cannot emulate.

14	N-B2	16 B-B4	B-Q2
15 QR-Q1	P-B3	17 BxN	

Strange! White gives up the "minor exchange" that Black had spurned. The idea, of course, is to destroy the piece that otherwise would have an unassailable post at K4 after White's next move.

17 . . .	RxB
18 P-B5	N-B1

VII-12   **After 18 . . . N-B1**

Despite the exchanges, the Black cramp begins to be serious. The knight has to go here to protect the QP, but then the QR is shut out of play.

19 P-K5!

The pawn must be captured, or else it goes on to K6, but QPxP loses the queen by N-K6ch.

19 . . .	BPxP
20 N-K6ch	BxN
21 PxB	R-K2

The object of 19 P-K5 is now clear: to open the file for the White rook. If 21 . . . RxRch 22 RxR followed by 23 R-B7ch, 24 Q-R6 and 25 Q-N7 mate.

22 Q-N5		Q-K1	

The mischief done by cutting off the QR ruins Black; could he play 22 . . . RxP, he would have a won game.

23 R-Q3	RxP	25 Q-R6ch	K-N1
24 R-R3	Q-K2	26 R-B8ch	QxR
		27 QxRP mate	

White can drift into a cramp through too lackadaisical opening moves. The following is a famous example of self-defeat.

ENGLISH OPENING

1 P-QB4	P-K3	3 P-K3	P-QB4
2 N-QB3	P-Q4	4 N-B3?	

P-Q4, which he might have played the previous move, was now imperative.

4 . . .	P-Q5!
5 N-K2	N-QB3
6 N-N3	P-KR4

That Black can afford the time for this advance underlines the losses of time by White.

7 P-QR3?	P-R5
8 N-K2	P-K4
9 P-Q3	P-R4

Curiouser and curiouser! Black still need not develop his pieces; he can occupy his time in forestalling White pawn advances.

10 P-R3	B-Q2
11 P-K4	P-B3
12 N-R2	P-KN4

Smothering White's last hope, P-KB4.

13 B-Q2	P-R5

VII-13   **After 13 . . . P-R5**

What a picture! Now White can do nothing but shuffle about in his little cave while Black plans a leisurely campaign to bore through the enveloping strata.

ORGANIC PAWN WEAKNESS

The pawn skeletons from an actual game are shown in Diagram VII-14. Here we see four features regarded as organic weaknesses:

VII-14   **Pawn Weaknesses**

Doubled pawns: two pawns of the same color on the same file, as White's pawns on the KB-file.

Isolated pawn: one incapable of protection by a friendly pawn on an adjacent file, as White's QP and KRP and Black's QRP.

Backward pawn: one not guarded by another and able to advance only at cost of attack by an enemy pawn, as the Black QBP.

Holes: squares on a player's 3rd rank, normally guarded by pawns, left unguarded by the advance of the adjacent pawns, as Black's KB3 and KR3.

The weakness of any such pawn formation will almost certainly be felt in an end game, that is, when the objective is to queen a pawn rather than to evolve a mating attack. In midgame, a formal pawn weakness may be irrelevant to the piece play. Often it is a cheap price paid for some advantage: e.g., allowing a doubled pawn opens a file for a rook. Sometimes it is even an advantage in itself, as when a wing pawn doubled toward the center fortifies control there.

The injunction is not, therefore, to avoid a pawn weakness at all costs but to weigh such a weakness against the possible gain. Do not let your pawn skeleton be ruined through sheer carelessness, but do not be afraid to pay for open lines, tempos in development, etc. We shall discuss these issues and cite examples.

Doubled Pawn. In Diagram VII-15, removal of the Black KNP has opened the file for an attack on the king. The doubled pawns

VII-15   Fatal Doubled Pawn

block the queen from defending K-side squares from Q2 or B2 and also impede the king's flight from the assailed sector. Verdict: the doubled pawns are a fatal weakness.

154 • Strategical Objectives: Part One

VII-16   Neutral Doubled Pawn

In Diagram VII-16, the doubling of the Black pawns has not split the pawn mass on the Q-side, so that there is no intrinsic weakness. Black has no center pawn to oppose the White KP; still, he can extend his control on the Q-file by P-QB4 and then possibly P-QB3. Finally, White has given up a bishop for a knight in doubling the pawn. Verdict: the doubled pawn is offset by compensating advantages.

In Diagram VII-17, Black's Q-side pawns are split, but the doubled pawn assures that Black can maintain a pawn at Q4 and a

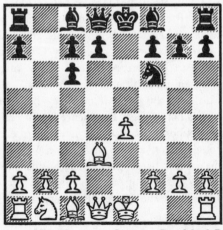

VII-17   Strong Doubled Pawn

pawn at QB3 to guard it. Thus he will obtain his fair share (or more) of center control. His bishops are unimpeded, and there is some prospect of putting the open QN-file to use. Verdict: the doubled pawns are strong.

Isolated Pawn. The intrinsic weakness of the "isolani" is that it can be guarded only by pieces. Its value depends on the present deployment and future prospects of the pieces on both sides. In

VII-18   **Weak Isolani**

Diagram VII-18, White has the means to blockade the isolani with the ideal piece, a knight: 1 N-QN3, B-N3 2 QN-Q4. (Blockade is often a necessary first step in attacking an isolani, so as to prevent its walking away from the attacks of knights and bishops.) White can later bring a rook to the file quickly by O-O-O and thus attack the pawn with at least two pieces, a rook and a knight. Black can apparently bring up an equal number of defenders: a knight at KB3, a rook at Q1, also a knight at K2 if need be—but merely to save the pawn from capture is not enough. Experience has shown that the attacker enjoys a greater opportunity than the defender to exert forks, swing his pieces to another sector, and so on. Here, White can supplement the attack on the isolani by advancing his K-side pawns, to menace, after O-O, both the Black king and an essential guard of the pawn (N at KB3). Verdict: the Black QP is very weak.

VII-19   **Weak Isolani**

Even when the isolani is safe from capture, it may be the most glaring symptom of an ill that is not at all its own fault but that of the rest of the army. In Diagram VII-19 the Black QP is heavily protected and not even attacked, yet it is fatally weak. What we really mean here is that Black is ruined by his inability to control the dark central squares. After 1 N-B5, Q-K2 2 B-N5, B-B3 3 Q-Q4, Black is so trussed up that he can scarcely move.

In Diagram VII-20, Black played 1 . . . PxP; White might have replied 2 NxP but instead played 2 PxP, deliberately giving himself

VII-20   **Strong Isolani**

an isolani. He argued that this pawn would be strong, for (a) it would allow N-K5 as soon as the Black knight moves (as it must to give scope to the other Black pieces); this outpost plus the other White pieces would keep Black so busy defending his K-side that he could not dream of massing against the isolani; and (b) the QP is passed and could not be quickly blockaded; Black would also have to defend against its advance to Q6 (supported by a rook), on which square it would be both secure and menacing. White's judgment was quickly corroborated. (2 . . . N-B3 3 KR-K1, Q-Q3 4 N-K5, P-QN4 5 B-N3, B-N2? 6 NxP, RxN 7 BxRch, KxB 8 Q-B7ch, Q-Q2 9 QxQch, NxQ 10 R-B7, B-B1 11 KR-QB1, and White wins the exchange.)

Backward Pawn. Like the isolani, the backward pawn may be a weakness because an attack upon it ties down pieces to its defense.

VII-21   Weak Backward Pawn

Diagram VII-21 is the typical outcome of a White Q-side "minority attack." The necessity of defending the weakling on QB3 prevents the Black pieces from getting into the open. White can utilize his greater space and mobility according to circumstances: to plant his QR on QB5 and then bring a pawn to Q5 to attack the pinned QBP once more (as by P-KB3, P-K4, etc.); or to advance his K-side pawns to open a file on that side after disposing his pieces to swing quickly over to an attack against the exposed Black king.

VII-22 Irrelevant Backward Pawn

At best, a backward pawn is neutral because irrelevant. In Diagram VII-22 (a continuation from Diagram VII-17), the Black pawn at QB3 is doubled as well as backward. Its weakness or strength, however, is beside the point: the game is going to be decided soon by the direct attacks against the kings. The Black king looks the more naked, yet it is the White that will be laid bare. (1 . . . P-R5 2 BxP, N-B6ch 3 PxN, QBxPch 4 B-N3, QxBch 5 PxQ, RxPch 6 K-R2, BxP 7 B-R3, RxBch 8 KxR, R-R1 mate.)

Holes. A hole is a square on your 3rd rank from which you cannot expel an enemy piece by a pawn. Now, manifestly, you cannot keep all your pawns at home: you are bound to advance some of them. Holes are necessarily created, but a square does not merit this reproachful term unless your opponent has real prospect of posting and maintaining a piece there in the teeth of your pieces.

Nominal holes are opened every time you fianchetto a bishop, yet this development is often strong: the bishop guards the holes and also bears offensively upon the center.

VII-23   **Queen-Side Hole**

In Diagram VII-23, Black moved 1 . . . B-R6 with the sequel 2 BxB, QxB. It may seem extraordinary that Black should want to exchange his "good" bishop for what looks like a "bad" bishop. But Black (world champion Capablanca) knows what he is about. He wants to restrain the White Q-side pawns and then attack them with the aid of a rook on his open QB-file. He can weaken the White QB pawn by swapping off the KB; nor can this pawn advance safely to QB4, for, after Black's PxP, the White center pawn (or pawns) would "dangle." It is true that all this lies in the remote future. After the further moves 3 QN-B3, B-Q2 4 NxN, BxN, White should have (the analysts say) moved 5 Q-B1, swapping or ousting the Black queen. If 5 . . . Q-N3, then 6 Q-Q2 or Q-N2. But White underestimated the danger, played 5 Q-Q2 and 6 P-B3, and the Black Q-side attack eventually won.

Holes are most serious when they lie in front of the castled king. Many instances can be seen in the diagram of other lessons, as VI-8 and VI-9. The danger is most extreme when the defensive bishop has been taken by a knight, leaving the enemy a bishop to exploit the holes.

VII-24   **White to Move**

But even after a bishop-for-bishop swap, a hole is a hole! In Diagram VII-24, White played 1 P-KB4, N-B3 2 BxB, KxB 3 Q-N2ch, P-B3 (forced), 4 P-KN4, and we can readily estimate that Black's weakness on KB3 must lose the game.

REVIEW VII

1. What is a phalanx?
2. What is a hole?
3. State two ways in which "pawn grabbing" may be dangerous?
4. What is a chain?
5. State two purposes served by the early advance of central pawns.
6. What is a subcenter pawn?
7. What precisely is meant by "control of the center"?
8. When a phalanx is opposed by a chain, what important option does the owner of the phalanx usually have?
9. What kind of move is always involved in "increasing your space" as we have used this expression?
10. State two circumstances in which you may well violate the old injunction, "Never move a piece twice in the opening until you have moved each piece once."

ANSWERS TO REVIEW VII

1. Two pawns on the same rank and adjacent files.
2. A 3rd-rank square not capable of being guarded by a pawn. (But this is called a hole only if the square is usually guarded by a pawn, and if there is a real prospect that the enemy can occupy or use it.)
3. Vital time may be lost from piece development, and the grabbing piece may fall into jeopardy.
4. Two pawns adjacent on a diagonal.
5. Gaining control of some central squares, opening lines for development of bishops, and expanding one's interior space.
6. A pawn on either bishop's file.
7. The ability to prevent enemy pieces from occupying central squares. (Your ulterior objective is, of course, to maintain one or more of your own pieces in the center, but, so long as you cannot do so, the center control is divided.)
8. To play PxP or to advance the unopposed pawn and form a chain himself.
9. A pawn move. We have defined "your space" as that behind your own pawns.
10. You may or must move a developed piece a second time (a) to avoid material loss, (b) to parry a threat in the most economical way, and (c) to take advantage of an enemy loss of time.

QUIZ VII

1. What is the most natural reply to (a) 1 P-QB4; (b) 1 P-KB4?
2. "Develop knights before bishops," is an old and untrustworthy maxim. Yet in most regular openings the last minor piece to be developed is a bishop. Why do you think this is so?

3 Black to move.

4 White to move.

3. The diagram shows a regular position of the *French Defense* in which Black has an "indicated" move. What do you think it is?

4. A "coffeehouse" opening is 1 P-K4, P-K4 2 B-B4, B-B4 3 P-Q4. What do you think White's plan is after 3 . . . PxP (Diagram)?

5 Black to move.

6 White to move and win.

5. In this position, would you consider P-Q5 a good move or a bad move. Why?

6. The diagram illustrates the disadvantages of a backward pawn in an endgame. What is the general plan for a White win?

7 White to move.

8 White to move.

7. In the diagrammed position, which side, if either, do you think is better developed?

8. Would you judge White's isolated QP in this position to be weak, strong, or neutral?

9 White to move.

10 White to move.

9. Here would you judge White's doubled QBP to be weak, strong, or neutral?

10. Would you judge White's doubled KBP to be weak, strong, or neutral?

11 White to move.

11. White's pawn structure has two formal weaknesses, the doubled pawn and the isolated pawn. Would you judge that these are likely to be a handicap, or fatal, or negligible?

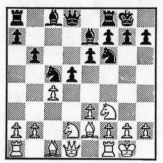

12(a) White to move.

12(b) White to move.

12. (a) Compare the development of both sides. Which, if either, do you think has the edge? (b) From Diagram (a) the actual continuation was:

1 PxP	NxP	4 Q-R4	Q-B3
2 N-N3	B-N2	5 B-R6	BxB
3 NxN	BxN	6 QxB	N-N5
	7 Q-K2		KR-Q1

The resulting position is shown in Diagram (b). Who has the edge in development now? Has there been a change? If so, what caused it?

ANSWERS TO QUIZ VII

1. (a) 1 . . . P-K4. (b) 1 . . . P-Q4. The most natural proced-
   ure is to advance a center pawn to the 4th rank if it will not be
   subject to attack and can be maintained there.

2. Because a bishop usually has more options for his first move
   than a knight. The short-stepping knight at the outset can usually
   do no more than strengthen the center, so that his choice is largely
   limited to B3 or a 2nd-rank square (Q2 or K2). The bishop
   can usually choose among several squares, on the diagonal toward
   the center, or N2 after P-N3. One of the better maxims of chess
   play is, "Reserve the option, when you can."

3. The indicated move is P-QB4. Black must try to smash the White
   pawn salient to escape a permanent cramp. The móve P-KB3
   also comes into consideration for this purpose and sometimes is
   a playable supplement to P-QB4, but in the given position the
   consequences of P-KB3, leaving the KP backward, are incalculable.
   The move P-QB4 hits at the base of the White pawn chain, does
   not weaken the Black pawn structure in any way, and paves the
   way for getting the QB into action.

4. The idea is 4 BxPch, KxB 5 Q-R5ch and 6 QxB. Thus White
   equalizes the material and deprives Black of the right to castle.

5. 1 . . . P-Q5 is undoubtedly the best move. It is true that by 2
   BxB, PxB White can give Black an isolated KP. (2 . . . NxB
   would be bad because of 3 Q-K4). But after the further moves
   3 PxP (practically forced), NxP 4 NxN, QxN, Black dominates
   the center, and his pieces are singularly hard to repel. (5 N-B3,
   Q-Q6! or 5 R-Q1, R-Q1.) Black has made a big step forward
   toward the capitalization of his Q-side pawn majority, and a
   White counterattack on the K-side has been slowed down by the
   opening of the KB-file for Black, which makes it more difficult
   for White to enforce P-KB4. In view of all this, Black's isolated
   KP is seen to be a negligible weakness. The pawn is shielded
   from frontal attack and does good service in defending Black's
   Q4 and KB4.

6. The general plan is to use White's K-side pawn majority, which
   is capable of generating a passed pawn, to hold the Black king
   on the K-side, while the White king goes over to the Q-side and
   captures both Black pawns there. Thus: 1 P-R5, K-B4 (by

K-Q4 Black can capture the White QNP, but White will get a queen in plenty of time to stop the Black Q-side pawns) 2 P-N6, PxP 3 PxP, KxP 4 K-K4, K-B3 5 K-Q5, K-K2 6 K-B6, K-Q1 7 K-N7, K-Q2 8 KxP, K-B2 9 K-R6, K-B1 10 KxP, K-N1. This position is a White win whichever player is to move (see Quiz III, Question 2).

7. Numerically, the development is equal: each side has four pieces off the back row, and it is White's move. Qualitatively, Black is ahead. His KB and KN are posted to threaten N-B5, compelling White to give up a bishop for a knight. The Black queen and QN prevent a counterattack by P-QB4. The White QN, though off the back row, is at the moment merely an obstruction. After he moves (to let the White queen guard KB4), Black can still enforce N-B5 by the preliminary Q-B2. (P-KN3 by White would incur a lasting pawn weakness on the K-side.)

8. In this lesson we remarked that the isolani "may be the most glaring symptom of an ill that is not at all its own fault." In the present position, we might credit the isolani with virtues not at all of its making. The White QP is here largely irrelevant. White has lashed down command of the QB-file, and his bishop hits the Black QNP. Black is going to be kept so busy defending himself against invasion that any attack on the White QP is a pipe dream. (White moved Q-B5, forcing an exchange of queens. Although an organic pawn weakness generally becomes more serious as an endgame approaches, White here has such a piece-superiority that he can loot the Black Q-side before Black can organize any counterplay in the center.)

9. The doubled pawn is weak, perhaps fatally. The square QB3 is "dead" to White; the pawn not only fights nothing but also interferes with the White communication between his wings. White's only hope is to mount a successful attack on the K-side, but here Black is well developed for defense. In the long run, White has to face a Black process (B-Q2, P-QN4) that will open a file for attack against his isolated QRP or his pawn on QB3.

10. The doubled pawn is not intrinsically weak, since the White pawns are not split (compare Diagram VII-16). The question is whether the pawn at KB3 can fight offensively better on that file than on the K-file. Since it can advance to B4 to command

K5 and since, if Black does not advance his KP to the 4th rank, his center remains cramped, we estimate that the White KP has gained rather than lost by being shunted to the KB-file. At present the White edge is slight, but it may increase if Black does not contrive to expand.

11. The White pawn weaknesses are very serious, since they leave the light squares on the K-side without pawn protection. Black, in fact, won this game by combining an attack against the king with threats against the QP, which can be defended only by pieces.

12. (a) The Black and White pieces are disposed symmetrically, except for the queen's knights. Here the difference is manifestly in Black's favor; his knight has reached a good 4th-rank post, whereas the White knight is on the 2nd rank and must be moved again to release the QB. White has lost his advantage of the first move—but no more. (Imagine the moves 1 P-QN3, PxP 2 NxP. The position is then wholly symmetrical, with Black to move. If White preserves his initial tempo, it will always be his turn in a wholly symmetrical position.)

(b) Black has four pieces in action; White has only two pieces off the back row. Thus Black has made a quantitative gain since position (a). He has gained even more qualitatively; he commands the open Q-file and can quickly reinforce and utilize that advantage (R-Q2, QR-Q1, N-Q6), while White cannot readily develop his Q-side (he cannot move B-Q2, P-QN3, nor R-N1).

The difference between (a) and (b) is due to the exchanges initiated by White. We see here three ways in which exchanges may lose time. (1) White's NxN exchanged a piece that had moved three times for one that had moved only twice. (2) This exchange improved the position of a Black piece, his KB. (3) The maneuver necessary to enforce the exchange of bishops brought the White queen in three moves (Q-R4-R6-K2) to a post that she could have reached in one.

Lesson VIII

STRATEGICAL OBJECTIVES: PART TWO

Let us continue the consideration of strategical objectives begun in Lesson VII. Our list of topics, in abbreviated terms, is:

General: Center Control
Development
Space   } Lesson VII
Pawn Weakness
King Safety

Specific: Outposts
File Opening
File Command
Mobile Pawn Wing
Minor Exchange

KING SAFETY

The question whether your king is safe depends, much of the time, on tactical details. General strategical considerations, however, will often save you from the need for tactical calculation.

A principle that is obvious but frequently overlooked is to keep watch of the offensive and defensive resources in your king's sector. Count the number of enemy pieces that bear upon it or that can quickly be brought to bear; compare that with the number of your own pieces near at hand. If your force is less, you had better calculate exactly what the enemy might do and what you should do to bolster your defense.

VIII-1   **Black to Move**

As in all departments of chess, here you will learn much from playing over master games. In particular, you will see the common patterns of attack and learn to recognize the characteristic positions that permit them. In Diagrams VI-10 and VI-11 we saw a type of position where the attackers include two bishops, a queen, and either a knight or a rook; the defenders are a knight and a bishop (plus what little help the KR can give). The sacrifice by BxRPch is standard. Now look at Diagram VIII-1. Its only major difference from the previous one is that although Black still has his defensive knight at KB3, this knight is already attacked by the White QB and can be attacked again by N-R5. After its disappearance, the White queen can sally to that key square of K-side attacks, KR5. Obviously Black must bolster his K-side in a hurry. Since he can swing none of his Q-side pieces over quickly, he had better attempt some such process as P-KN3, N-K1, P-B3 or B-B3. Now, we are not concerned with whether this defense is adequate (probably it is not), but with the extraordinary fact that Black did not perceive his peril! He moved 1 . . . P-QR3, then 2 N-R5 (of course!) NxN? (the last hope was N-K1) 3 BxPch, KxB 4 QxNch, K-N1 5 BxP, KxB 6 Q-N4ch, K-R2 7 R-B3, etc.

The question of where to put your king in the first place is strategical. We may say that O-O is the "normal" course, because it is indicated in many thoroughly analyzed opening variations. The alternative O-O-O is good only in rather special circumstances; novices tend to play O-O-O too freely.   Still, in an uncommon position the choice must be based on its merits, not on prejudice.

VIII-2   **White to Move**

In Diagram VIII-2, the time has come when White must decide where to put his king.   Against O-O is the obvious menace of Black's open KN-file and his mighty bishop.   Against O-O-O is the ragged state of the Q-side pawns.   Against keeping the king in the center is the difficulty of then getting the KR into play. White correctly chooses the least hazardous course by 1 O-O-O.   Black now has an easy decision: O-O is unthinkable, for all five White pieces plus his K-side pawns could then combine in a smashing attack against the king; O-O-O is safe because Black's Q-side is strongly guarded by his pieces and intact pawns there.

VIII-3   **White to Move**

In Diagram VIII-3, Black has already advanced on the K-side to such an extent that O-O by White would be "castling into it." Should White keep O-O-O in reserve by leaving his QR unmoved? The player (Petrosian) judged that it was worth abandoning this resource to use the QR on the Q-side; he moved 1 R-QN1. His king was never in danger but was repeatedly an obstruction, wherefore it moved at separate intervals to Q2, B1, N2, and R1. White won the game.

After 1 R-QN1, Black had to make a decision on the defense of his QNP: P-N3, O-O-O, or R-QN1? Against P-N3 is the certainty that by P-QR4-R5 (with due preparation) White can saddle Black with either an isolated QRP or a backward QNP, either of which would almost surely cost Black a pawn. Against O-O-O is the nakedness of the Black king: e.g., 1 . . . O-O-O 2 Q-N3, P-N3 3 P-QR4, etc. Black therefore moved 1 . . . R-QN1. Then 2 B-K3, and again Black was faced with the problem of where to put his king—since it looks as if he cannot move forward until he connects his rooks. Against 2 . . . O-O is the displacement of the KR, which is wanted on the K-side to support the general advance there. Black actually chose 2 . . . K-Q1 and 3 . . . K-B2, using his king to bolster his Q-side—with the result that the king got into trouble there. We conclude that, if Black cannot leave his king on K1, or move K-B1-N2, then his early advance on the K-side is unsound.

THE OUTPOST

In its narrowest sense, an outpost is a knight on the 5th or a more advanced rank, established on a square from which he cannot be expelled by an enemy pawn and where he is himself guarded by a pawn. In its broadest sense, an outpost is a piece established on a square from which it normally would be excluded by an enemy or a friendly pawn.

We think of a knight, more than of any other piece, as an outpost because he must come close to the enemy to bear upon him, unlike a bishop, rook, or queen, who can operate from a distance.   In Diagram

VIII-4   **Black to Move**

VIII-4, Black played 1 . . . N-N1, a move that looks like willful "undevelopment" but is explained by the subsequent tour N-K2-B3-Q5. Here the knight bores into the White camp and if captured is replaced by a pawn that commands vital squares on White's 3rd rank. Had White recognized the menace of the outpost (this game was played in 1873), he would have moved the QN away and P-QB3 to exclude the knight; instead he let the knight come in and died of strangulation (Anderssen versus Steinitz, both world champions).

VIII-5   *Pillsbury Attack*

The existence or creation of squares for outposts depends on the pawn structure. The nature of pawn moves is such that you have to "give to get," since every advancing pawn commands new squares but abandons old ones. Establishing a station for an outpost usually involves conceding another station to your opponent. The crucial question is: which station is the more valuable? We can only direct your attention to this question; we cannot supply the answer. Diagram VIII-5 is the "set position" that White strives for in the *Pillsbury Attack* in the *Queen's Gambit Declined*. To fortify his knight at K5, White has left his own K4 open to invasion, so that, after 1 . . . N-K5 2 BxB, QxB, White is more or less forced to continue 3 BxN, since the Black outpost cannot be expelled by a pawn while White's knight has to face P-KB3. (3 QNxN, PxN leaves White's KB dead.) Now the question is: whose attack gets there first, White's on the K-side or Black's on the Q-side? Do not despair if you cannot answer this question offhand—most of the early analysts were wrong about it! We merely wish to point out by this example that the establishment of advanced posts for your pieces is often fraught with long-term strategical considerations.

FILE OPENING

A player is said to have a *half-open file* when his pawn has disappeared from it but the enemy pawn has not. A rook on such a file may exert strong pressure on the enemy camp as well as guard one's advanced pieces. A frequent midgame objective is therefore to open a file for one's rooks. White may declare this purpose as early as his second move: 1 P-K4, P-K4 2 P-KB4. The idea of the *King's Gambit* is to press through the KB-file to Black's weak spot, his KB2.

VIII-6 **White to Move**

The half-open KB-file is the basis for numerous patterns of K-side attack, as many examples in these lessons show. Diagram VIII-6 is one instance. At the cost of a pawn, White has obtained two bishops against two knights, and has created a breach in the enemy K-side. "Black's dark squares are somewhat weak now—but his knight at K1 is a stout defender." (Alekhine) White, indeed, must quickly find something to offset Black's infiltration on the Q-side. So: 1 P-B4! "The opening of this file offers fair equalizing prospects—but with right answers hardly more."

The game continued: 1 . . . KPxP 2 QxP, PxP 3 PxP, R-B6 4 Q-B2, N-K3? (Alekhine recommends N-QB3) 5 P-QR4, QR-B1 6 R-KB1 (threatens 7 BxRP), R6-B2 7 R-N1, Q-B3 8 P-R5. "Incredible but true—White has suddenly obtained a strong pressure on the queen's side." The threat is, of course, 9 R-N6 and capture of the QRP. Black moved 8 . . . N-B4, whereupon his K-side collapsed: 9 B-QB4, Q-Q2 10 Q-R2! Black can bring no additional guard to his KB2, nor is N-K3 feasible, because repeated captures on that square would open the way for the White KR to reach B8 with mate. Black must give up his queen for two pieces—but then he loses the knight also: 10 . . . NxP 11 RxP, QxR 12 BxQch, RxB 13 Q-K6, Resigns.

VIII-7   **Black to Move**

In many variations of the Queen's Pawn Opening, it is the QB-file that is first half-opened. Diagram VIII-7 typifies the perennial Black problem of how to develop his QB. One try is 1 . . . P-QN3 to fianchetto the bishop. But with 2 PxP, PxP White trains his guns on the QBP. Whether it is left at home or advanced to B3 or B4, Black has a pawn on the open file that can be defended only by pieces —a weakness that often proves fatal.

An interesting illustration of the dominating role that may be played by half-open files arose from Diagram VIII-8. The square Q5

VIII-8   **White to Move**

"beckons" to the White knight, since Black dare not play P-K3 leaving his QP backward on the open file. White could keep the upper hand by 1 Q-Q3 (to parry the threat of NxP), by developing his rooks on Q1 and K1, by taking any necessary measures to combat the attempt by Black to attack the Q-side through the QB-file, and by moving N-Q5 only when the capture of this outpost would be as bad for Black as letting it remain. Instead, White thought to clear away all the obstacles at one stroke: 1 P-K5? BxB 2 KxB, N-K1 3 Q-K4 (otherwise Black gets rid of his weak QP by P-Q3), R-B1 4 B-N5, P-B3. Now the seamy side of 1 P-K5 shows up—Black gets a half-open file for his other rook, too. 5 PxP, NxP 6 Q-K2, R-B3 7 QR-Q1, Q-R1 8 K-N1, R-K3 9 Q-Q3, R-Q3. Thanks to the QB-file, Black was able to bring this rook in front of his center pawns and harry the dominating queen. 10 Q-B2, RxR 11 RxR, Q-B3 12 P-N3, P-K3. What is this? Can Black leave his QP backward just to exclude the White knight? But Black has reckoned that there will be no backward pawn. By his pin on the QB-file he threatens P-Q4, establishing an isolated but very lively passed pawn. Necessary was 13 BxN, BxB, but Black could still enforce P-Q4, preceded if necessary by BxN. Instead: 13 Q-Q3, N-N5! (Diagram VIII-9) Now Black shows

VIII-9   After 13 . . . N-N5!

his fangs, and the KB-file suddenly comes to life. 14 B-B4, P-KN4! 15 P-B3, Q-B4ch 16 K-N2, Q-B7ch 17 K-R3, QxRPch 18 KxN, RxBch 19 Resigns, for he is mated on the next move.

The power of a rook in backing up attacks through an open file has been abundantly illustrated in Lesson VI. We need only to point out that, once a file is completely opened, you should weigh the urgency of bringing a rook quickly to it, either to gain command of it or to prevent the enemy from doing so.

VIII-10   **The Open File**

In the schematic Diagram VIII-10, the player to move has an advantage possibly sufficient to win. For example: 1 QR-B1, QR-B1 (surely he must oppose the penetration of the White rook) 2 R-B5. The pawn configuration is such that the White rook can advance in the teeth of the Black in order to double the rooks. If 2 . . . RxR 3 QPxR, the protected passed pawn on the side remote from the Black king is probably more than Black can survive. White thus gains space for 3 KR-B1, after which his command of the file is indisputable. He can harry the Black pawns from B7 or B6, tying down the Black pieces to their defense, while his own king advances to support pawn advances that will open further avenues of approach. Either before or after a general swap of rooks, the White king will go raiding among the Black pawns.

VIII-11   Danger of File Opening

The battle for an open file is not often so tactically simple. Diagram VIII-11 is a regular position of the *Queen's Gambit Declined*. Black's perennial problem is that to get his QB into action he must enforce either P-K4 or P-QB4. The latter move has been tried in this position: 1 . . . P-QB4 2 PxQP, PxQP 3 NxP, PxP. Black has submitted to an isolated QP, but it cannot be effectively attacked for some time; his greater danger is from the open file. After five further moves we reach Diagram VIII-12, and it is clear that Black has not the means to dispute White's command of the QB-file.

VIII-12   Indisputable File Command

His rook is tied to the defense of the QRP. The naive P-QR3 would allow Q-N6, whereupon the White queen would attack the QNP and also command all the dark squares in the Black camp. Nor can Black hope to close the file by B-B3, for even if he could bring additional support to that square (as by Q-Q3) he would have to answer NxB by PxN, leaving his Q-side pawns even weaker than before. It is noteworthy that among the evils facing him, Black chose the surrender of the QRP as the least. (9 P-QR3, P-KN3 10 P-R3, R-QB1 11 RxRch, BxR 12 QxRP. White—world champion Alekhine—overestimated the ease of winning this "won game" and let Black escape with a draw!)

VIII-13 Rook on the Seventh Rank

"The ultimate triumph of the open file," it has been said, "is to get a rook to the 7th rank." From this post the rook attacks the enemy pawn base and may also menace the king. An instance is Diagram VIII-13. White has been outplayed and has left his 2nd rank open to invasion. The reckoning comes swiftly: 1 . . . R-B7 2 B-R3, P-K5 3 QR-N1 (unhappily he cannot play QR-B1 because of the fork N-K7ch), P-K6! 4 PxP, RxKP 5 R-KB1, RxPch 6 K-R1, R-R6, Resigns, since he is mated on the next move.

A mating attack against the castled king usually requires the advance of one or more pawns on the side to which the king has castled

VIII-14   **The Pawn Storm**

to make a breach in the defending pawns. A typical "pawn storm" ensued from Diagram VIII-14:

	1 P-KB4	P-KB4

The pawn must vacate KB2 to give space for pieces to come to the defense, but, of course, KN3 is weakened. At the moment, this square is not even attacked and it is overprotected, but watch the defense crumble!

	2 P-KR3	N-Q2
	3 K-R2	P-B4

Black strives for counterplay and would get it if White would kindly play PxP, but, of course, White keeps the center closed.

	4 P-B3	P-B5
	5 B-QB2	P-QR3
	6 N-B3	P-R3

This move, further weakening KN3, is intrinsically undesirable but unavoidable; to permit 7 N-N5 would be ruinous.

7 P-KN4

The steamroller comes on!

7 . . .	K-R2	9 Q-K1	N-QB3?
8 R-KN1	R-KN1	10 N-R4	Q-KB1

VIII-15   After 10 . . . Q—KB1

11 NxNP

Little calculation is needed to see that this sacrifice is sound. If 11 . . . KxN 12 PxPch and 13 PxP, White is left with two connected pawns that can be supported by no less than six pieces. White can expect to win back two pieces (one for each pawn) and emerge material ahead—even if there is no quick mate (as there was).

Observe in the foregoing that the advance of the Black pawns on the K-side (P-KB4, P-KR3) weakened his defense, whereas the White pawn advances strengthened his attack without jeopardizing his king at all. Here is an anomaly that needs explanation! This is to be found in the initial superiority of the White position in two essential respects: (a) He has greater space to maneuver because of his advanced center pawns and is thus able to poise more pieces for attack than Black can bring up for defense; and (b) the center is stabilized and cannot be cracked open. Black has no avenue of approach to the denuded White king.

The novice is inclined to make too many pawn moves in the opening. That is why we have emphasized that every early pawn move is, in effect, a tempo lost from piece-development. Nevertheless, there may be time for space-gaining pawn advances if the enemy develops too lackadaisically, especially if he lets the center go by default. Here is a game in point:

PETROFF DEFENSE

1 P-K4	P-K4	3 NxP	P-Q3
2 N-KB3	N-KB3	4 N-KB3	NxP
	5 P-Q4		

VIII-16   **After 5 P—Q4**

The usual move now is 5 . . . P-Q4, and Black can develop as rapidly as White. Instead, Black tries a strategic plan based on keeping pawn control over his K4.

5 . . .	B-K2	7 O-O	O-O
6 B-Q3	N-KB3	8 P-KR3	

At the time this game was played (1898), P-KR3 to prevent the pin of the KN was in bad repute. The pawn may become a target of attack. But here the move contributes to White's counterplan—to restrict the scope of the Black pieces.

8 . . .   B-K3

9 P-B4

More of the same! White can take the time for these pawn moves because his development is qualitatively superior.

9 . . .   P-B3

The Black QN cannot yet come out at B3 or Q2, since in either case P-Q5 would win a piece.

10 N-N5

To let his KBP advance. It is, of course, extraordinary that

White can afford to move a developed piece twice more to mobilize a mere pawn!

10	. . .	N-R3

If 10 . . . P-KR3, 11 NxB, and the light squares in the Black camp become woefully weak.

11	N-QB3	N-B2
12	P-B4	

VIII-17   **After 12 P—B4**

Restive under the cramp, Black now tries to precipitate 13 NxB, for then perhaps he can later smash the White center by P-K4, but White does not oblige.

12	. . .	P-KR3	14	Q-B2	R-N1
13	N-B3!	Q-B1	15	P-KB5	B-Q2
	16	B-B4		P-QN4	

Black strikes back where he can, but cannot shake off White's grip on the center.

17	P-QN3	P-B4	19	N-K2	P-QR4
18	P-Q5	P-N5	20	P-N4	

VIII-18   **After 20 P–N4**

Here we draw the veil on Black's suffering. The tremendous White pawn salient is the sort of thing on which money is borrowed from a bank. A concluding plan for White is 21 K-R2, followed by R-KN1-2 and QR-KN1 and the smashing open of the KN-file by P-N5. The preponderance of the White force in the enemy camp is overwhelming.

THE MINOR EXCHANGE

The bishop and knight are rated approximately equal. Nevertheless, in particular positions, one piece or the other is likely to be the more useful, and in most cases it is the bishop that is so favored. Therefore, to capture a bishop for a knight is considered "winning the *minor exchange*." The knight has the advantage over the bishop that he can attack both light and dark squares; but the bishop can operate from a distance, can attack widely separated points simultaneously, and can maneuver much more rapidly. Observe how these factors ultimately decide the following game.

VIII-19   **White to Move**

In Diagram VIII-19, White sees that the Black knight has a strong post in prospect at Q4 (to oust it by P-QB4 would leave the White QP too weak). His own bishop seems merely to duplicate the work of his center pawns; therefore, 1 BxN. A strategic mistake! Now White has the task of keeping the important diagonals closed lest the Black bishop get free play.

VIII-20   **White to Move**

The ensuing play up to Diagram VIII-20 demonstrated not so much the superiority of the bishop as the inferiority of the White player. The bishop was in fact a mere spectator while the other Black pieces maneuvered patiently in an effort to enforce P-K4. White did not realize that he should keep his knight on KB3 to oppose this advance but blithely swung it into the station QB5. Here it looks strong, but it is in fact weak. Black threatens to win a pawn by PxP, but White cannot himself play PxP because of QxN. Therefore:

1 N-N7	R-K1	3 Q-B3	Q-K2
2 PxP	R(1)xP	4 RxR	PxR
	5 N-R5		

The bishop comes to life, preventing 5 RxP, for then would follow RxR 6 QxR, Q-K8ch 7 K-R2, B-K4ch 8 P-N3, QxPch 9 Q-N2, BxPch, etc.

5 . . .	R-K8ch
6 RxR	QxRch
7 K-R2	P-Q5

Thanks to the long-range bishop, Black can now trade off his isolated pawn. Still more, he splits the White pawns and thereby wins one of them.

8 N-B6	PxP
9 PxP	BxP

VIII-21   **After 9 . . . BxP**

Now White cannot regain his pawn by 10 NxP because of B-Q5 (the forking power of the bishop!). It is true that Black would not thereby threaten to win the knight (after BxN White has the return fork Q-N8ch), but he would threaten BxP, after which mate by Q-KN8 could not be stopped. White would have to play (after 10 ... B-Q5) 11 P-N3, BxP 12 Q-N2 to guard the mate square. Then comes 12 ... P-R5! 13 PxP, Q-K4ch 14 K-R1, BxN, and Black does win the knight because 15 Q-N8ch is met by Q-N1. Again the rapid action of the bishop triumphs.

REVIEW VIII

1. What is meant by "winning the *minor exchange*"?
2. What is a half-open file?
3. What piece is the strongest single defender of the castled king?
4. "You have to give to get" has particular reference to what?
5. When may a player be said to "command" an open file?
6. In what respects is a bishop superior to a knight?
7. In a particular position where a knight is superior to a bishop, what is (most probably) the reason?
8. Why is a knight used for an outpost more frequently than any other piece?
9. In what two ways does a rook on the 7th rank usually exert its power?
10. State two conditions that normally must be fulfilled if a player is to attack by advancing his pawns in front of his castled king without serious jeopardy to his own king.

ANSWERS TO REVIEW VIII

1. Capturing a bishop at the cost of a knight.
2. A file is half-open to a player whose pawn has disappeared from it, while the enemy pawn has not.
3. A knight at B3.
4. Pawn advances. Any pawn advance establishes command of new squares but relinquishes guard of others.
5. When he has a rook (or queen) on the file that cannot be safely opposed by an enemy rook (or queen).
6. The bishop operates at long range, commands widely separated squares, and maneuvers much faster. Another point, not men-

tioned in the lesson, is that, if a bishop must withdraw for his own safety, he can still maintain essential guard of a focal square.

7. Probably that the knight can reach and attack both light and dark squares, whereas the bishop is tied to one color.

8. Because the knight operates at short range. He must reach an advanced post to strike at the enemy camp.

9. By attacking the base of the enemy pawns and by menacing the enemy king.

10. The player must have initial superiority in development (especially in his ability to bring more pieces quickly to the attack than the enemy can muster for defense), and the center must be stabilized, so that the enemy cannot outflank the advancing pawn wing and bring his pieces to bear on the denuded king.

QUIZ VIII

1. State two circumstances, in either of which O-O-O may be preferable to O-O.

2 White to move. **3** Black to move.

2. In this regular position of the *Sicilian Defense* the usual move is 1 B-K2. What do you think is the particular purpose in placing this bishop at K2 instead of B4 (which is a good alternative)?

3. In this position, Black played 1 . . . BxN and White replied 2 PxB. What reasons do you think prompted this recapture instead of BxB?

4 White to move.

5 White to move.

4. White can quickly establish a strategical advantage. How?

5. A certain White maneuver is "indicated." What is it?

6 White to move.

7 Black to move.

6. White played 1 N-B4. What do you think is the *strategic* purpose of this move?

7. Black moved 1 . . . P-QN4, and the move was awarded an exclamation point by the analysts. What purposes does this move serve?

8 White to move.   **9** White to move.

8. White moved 1 Q-B6. (a) Why does White want to exchange queens? What will he do after 1 . . . QxQ? (b) Can Black safely reply 1 . . . N(4)-K3?

9. The sequel from this position was 1 B-K4, B-N4 2 KR-K1, Q-Q3 3 BxN, PxB. Do you think White has gained or lost by this maneuver?

10 Black to move.

10. What would you advise for Black: O-O, O-O-O, or some other move? What are the most important factors to be considered?

ANSWERS TO QUIZ VIII

1. The K-side pawns are split or otherwise impaired so that they would not sufficiently shelter the king after O-O, or the K-side pawns can be effectively advanced for attack, and the player does not want to put his king in the way of the pieces backing them up.

2. The natural post for the QB is K3, but, if at once B-K3, Black

can move N-KN5 and either win the minor exchange or compel a bishop to move again. The purpose of 1 B-K2 is to forestall N-N5.

3. By BxB White could retain the possibility of later moving P-K4, P-KB4, and P-K5. This is a long-winded process, which has to reckon with (a) the tactical consequences of such Black maneuvers as N-KR4 and QN-Q2-B4 and (b) the strategic possibility that Black might be able to plant and maintain a pawn at his K4. By PxB White ensures that the Black KP cannot safely advance (in the teeth of White's immediate R-K1 and P-B4). White judges that prolongation of the Black cramp is the surer road to victory.

The capture PxB seems to hamper one White bishop or the other, whether the pawn is left on B3 or moved to B4. This is not true, however, for the QB does not want to go to N5. His proper place is in opposition to the Black bishop, by B-K3-Q4 or P-N3 and B-N2.

4. 1 BxN, PxB 2 BxB, PxB 3 P-B4. On the 3rd rank the pawns "dangle," and the Black king is left somewhat exposed. White can immediately open the KB-file for attack. Clearly Black is going to be hard put to defend both his king and the displaced pawns.

5. The "indicated" maneuver is N-K2-Q4. On this unassailable square the knight (a) blocks the QP, (b) reaches into enemy territory, (c) supports P-KB5 in the remote future, and (d) guards QB2 at home. Oddly enough, as the game developed, (d) proved to be most important of these factors.

6. To divert the KBP to the K-file, thus leaving the light squares around the Black king very weak and possibly saddling Black with a backward pawn. This came to pass: 1 . . . QR-Q1? 2 NxN, PxN 3 B-N6, R-K2 4 P-B4! (Black should have tried 1 . . . R-K2 so that, if 2 NxN, PxN 3 B-N6, he could immediately move 3 . . . P-K4!)

7. The move gains space on the Q-side. An important immediate effect is to allow Q-N3; from there the queen is much more active than she would be on Q2 after the advance of the QP. Later, Black may continue with P-QR4 and may threaten a breakthrough by a further advance of the phalanx. As the game went, this threat of invasion on the Q-side drew so much of the White

force there that Black (having greater space) was able to switch suddenly to a successful K-side mating attack!

Observe that Black can take the time for the "unnecessary" pawn move 1 . . . P-QN4 because (a) he is actually a tempo ahead in piece development and (b) he need not hurry to advance his QP. It does not block his pieces, and, as long as he retains the option of P-Q3 or P-Q4, any White plan has to reckon with this option.

8. (a) White wants to exchange queens to capitalize on his command of the K-file. After 1 . . . QxQ 2 NxQch, K-R1 3 R-K7, Black can never challenge the file by R-K1 until he succeeds in ousting the White knight. (b) The effort to close the file by 1 . . . N(4)-K3 fails through 2 N-R6ch, K-R1 3 NxPch forcing RxN because 3 . . . K-N1 4 NxQ, RxQ 5 NxN would cost a piece.

9. White has gained because he is now sure of commanding the QB-file and of getting a rook to the 7th rank. The actual continuation was 4 Q-R5, P-QR3 5 Q-B7! (Compare Diagram VIII-12.) White's judgment in destroying the knight at Q4 was praised, since in many positions the investment of the minor exchange for this purpose is a net loss.

10. Against 1 . . . O-O is the circumstance that 2 BxN, PxB wrecks the K-side pawns. However, this transaction has its bright side: White gives up the minor exchange, the rank is opened for guard of KR2 by the queen (this pawn is threatened as soon as White makes the routine developing move Q-B2), and possibly Black may mount a counterattack through the half-open file (K-R1, R-KN1, Q-N2).

Against 1 . . . O-O-O is the fact that White already has a pawn storm under way on that side (P-B5, P-QR4, P-N5, or the immediate P-N5). This attack is the more forceful if it also involves a hazard for the Black king, since it cannot be halted; it can only be offset, if at all, by counterattack in another sector.

The natural reaction to the wing attack is a center break, but Black is ill-prepared for P-K4, having both his queen and king on the file. White, indeed, threatens to make trouble in the center himself by R-K1 and possibly P-Q5. It seems imperative for Black to get at least his king off the file soon.

This appraisal apparently indicates that Black has a bad game, and this is the fact! He has no good moves, only some less hopeless than others.

Most hopeless, surely, is O-O-O (the player's actual choice), since White then has an easy course. (A player with the inferior game should seek complications in which his opponent might go astray.) The move O-O is hazardous but offers some prospect of enabling Black to hit back either in the center or on the K-side. If Black is to delay castling, the indicated move is surely N-B2, avoiding disruption of his pawns and preparing P-K4. Either O-O or N-B2 would be a rational choice.